TH

GOLDEN LADDER

RISE TO

BE UNSTOPPABLE

VIJAY PARTHASARATHY

Clever Fox
PUBLISHING

Chennai • Bangalore

CLEVER FOX PUBLISHING
Chennai, India

Published by CLEVER FOX PUBLISHING 2023

ISBN: 978-93-56481-70-1

International Praise
for
THE
GOLDEN LADDER
RISE TO
BE UNSTOPPABLE

"In my long corporate career, I was exposed to the wisdom of many business leaders. I was fortunate to learn from leading consultants and business school professors. They helped me understand the leadership and managerial skills required to lead a sizeable multinational operation.

"*THE GOLDEN LADDER, RISE TO BE UNSTOPPABLE* is a unique, outstanding summary of all the forty years that I spent learning and practising. Vijay has done a fabulous job of sharing secrets of success in a simple and engaging writing style with examples from the real world, which shows the significant number of leaders and brands who have implemented the ideas he shared. I loved how he explains complex concepts like *vision* and *strategy* in easy-to-understand language and how any business can create its own vision and strategy to win.

"I believe the book will be an excellent guide for all entrepreneurs and business leaders to help them win their customers and dominate the markets with their products and services. I wish I had the opportunity to read such a book early in my career!

"I thank Vijay Parthasarathy for sharing his years of experience and wisdom, which will benefit millions of leaders and professionals in the coming months.

"I look forward to his next book."

–NARENDRA AMBWANI

Former Managing Director, Johnson & Johnson Ltd.

"Much has been written in the past about the art and science of management leading to learning and tool kits. A book that provokes thought, which is a rare commodity today. And that makes you want to read through it as Vijay throws at you the idea of the Golden Ladder. The science is persuasive and the examples inspiring. It is well worth a read, even if you do NOT want to climb the corporate ladder. It is plainly and simply alluring."

–BHASKAR BHAT
Chairman, Vistara Airlines;
Former MD, TITAN Industries; Board Member Tata Sons

"I am pleased to see Vijay coming up with a book describing his observations over a long period about business success. Vijay is passionate about making a difference and has never given less than 100 percent to whatever he puts his mind. Wish him and his book all the success."

–BHARAT PATEL
Former Chairman and Managing Director,
Procter & Gamble, India

"The power of the mind makes the difference in how life unfolds at the professional and personal level. Vijay synthesises his 40-plus years of corporate and life learnings eloquently into this easy-to-read book bound to trigger meaningful dialogue and reflection."

–JAY JAYARAMAN
Former Managing Director,
Colgate-Palmolive India, Ltd.

"Awesome subject. Excellent and simple articulation of stories of innovation and excellence backed by a practical set of tools, behaviour and mindset needed to make this happen. A very timely guide for any individual aspiring to personal and professional nirvana. Vijay has first-hand experience of the magic of working with legends. So, when he speaks, it is helpful we listen."

–SANJEEB CHAUDHURI
Chairman, IDFC First Bank, Former CEO, Citibank EMEA and Global Head,
Global Mentor, Columbia Business School

"This book brings to life all the learnings and wisdom of Vijay which can be easily adopted and executed in real-life situations... one of the most interesting, practical and readable books for all practitioners and students of transformative leadership. An absolute must-read."

–SUPRATIM BOSE

Former Company Group Chairman,

Johnson & Johnson Medical Devices & Diagnostics;

President APMEA, Boston Scientific Corp.

"This book is a breath of fresh air, bringing new insights to the Brand and Business Strategy field. Vijay has deep knowledge and experience in dealing with the world's best brands, but what makes this book special is his personal touch. Drawing on his own experience with great honesty, he has created a powerful toolkit that will allow the reader to 'RISE TO BE UNSTOPPABLE'. That is the hallmark of great brands, companies and marketers."

–MICKY PANT

Former CEO, Yum Restaurants International (KFC, Pizza Hut)

"Eminently qualified, thanks to his personal experiences, Vijay describes the principles of achieving 'legendariness', how brand legends were made and survived onslaughts, including pandemics. The book is written in a breezy style, yet with conceptual depth. And then the intense idea of reprogramming the subconscious! A rich reflection piece to enable those who are willing to dream, thereby Rising and being UNSTOPPABLE."

–Dr G. RAGHURAM

Former Director, IIM Bangalore

"Vijay has aptly captured a practical, insightful roadmap to creating successful businesses and people relationships - the ability to withstand adversity and emerge a winner! Ultimately, there is no substitute for the power of the MIND, the QUALITY of THINKING and the ability to create BALANCE in all we do. This is what leads to transformation."

–SURESH GOKLANEY

Former Vice-Chairman & MD, Eureka Forbes Ltd.

"The history of modern corporations is replete with stories of companies that built spectacularly successful businesses over a decade or two. But only a few great companies, some with seemingly simple business models, prosper and endure for scores of years. If you have ever pondered these mysteries of the business world, ***this book is a must-read.*** *Vijay Parthasarathy, in his inimitable style, helps us unravel the secret of the Golden Ladder that enables these select companies to scale unimaginable heights. Vijay's narrative makes it clear that there is more to it than a compelling business model or an impregnable moat. It has everything to do with the mind."*

–Dr RAMASASTRY AMBARISH

Chairman and Dean, MYRA School of Business

"In the book RISE TO BE UNSTOPPABLE, Vijay looks at successful companies through his Golden Ladder prism. He identifies key lessons that can enable a company to survive the toughest of times and come back stronger. He uses his four decades of experience across multiple companies, countries and brands to draw some essential lessons. A ***highly engaging read*** *to prepare for the volatile tomorrows."*

–AMBI PARAMESWARAN

Author,Former Executive Director, CEO, FCB ULKA Advertising

"Having known Vijay since IIT days, I can vouch for his restless, creative mind, his out-of-the-ordinary, unconventional approach and immense passion. This book draws on a science and his rich, practical experience of implementing that science. ***A must-read."***

–JAYANT BHAT

President, Scotwork, India

"What I have admired most about Vijay, a well-known speaker, is how he has seamlessly moved in life, leveraging his knowledge and synthesising the success framework and sharing how each of us can use it in our careers. I am glad he has now converted this wisdom into a book that has significant relevance for start-ups and other companies in today's times bordering on multiple challenges. Recommend reading and practising all the success mantras encapsulated in the book."

–ARVIND MAHAJAN

Former Partner and Senior Director, KPMG Board

"I am happy to see Vijay bringing out this book to share all that he knew, observed, felt, experienced and advised after having dealt with several businesses and brands.

Who else can bring out these nuggets of wisdom? He has had long experience and built brands and businesses for those whom he describes as 'legends'. I personally feel that **this book should stand apart** *because it combines the recipe for successful businesses by following the best management practices. But more than that, it covers the secret recipes of the mind. So, I call this book a* **Business or Brand Metaverse**. *In his book, Vijay has created a platform for businesses and brands to develop and grow not only through physical reality but also through immersive experiences by sharing stories from several brands across varied business landscapes. He describes the known and the unknown through lucid analysis.*

"I feel that this book will be a compendium for management students to learn what's not normally taught in management schools and for brand marketers and business leaders to take their businesses to greater heights and make it to the list of legends."

–SATISH KUMAR ANAVANGOT

Former Managing Director, Henkel India Ltd.

"Vijay has elegantly explained the sound principles of management and the attitudinal aspects of successful business leaders. He has brilliantly covered the real-life stories of how successful business leaders took critical decisions in unstructured situations. **A must-read for budding entrepreneurs** *and professional managers aspiring to get to the top of the ladder in their careers."*

–L. RAMKUMAR

Former Managing Director, Tube Investments (India) Ltd.

" To relentlessly travel the road less travelled, to scale new heights continually, Vijay has practised and achieved what he preaches in his book. This is rare and makes me believe that **every page will ring true** *and the reader will unearth nuggets of actionable insights in every chapter.* ***A new success mantra awaits!***"

–NITEEN BHAGWAT

Former Vice-Chairman FCB. ULKA; Director, Karira Consulting

"Vijay brings to his readers nuggets from the wealth of his experience in building powerful brands and organisations that offer both practical guidance and invaluable insights. He suggests how leaders at all levels can synergise their domain expertise and knowledge with the often ignored but fantastic power that the human mind can bring to bear.

"Vijay overcame major personal challenges many of us would have failed to recover from. His learnings from working on harnessing the capacity of his mind to overcome barriers and reimagine opportunities can help all of us become better leaders and human beings. His book provides techniques and habits that will be valuable to all aspiring managers and leaders."

–RAVI MENON

Former Managing Director, India & SE Asia, Allergan Ltd.

"Vijay in his book expertly straddles the two powerful engines of strong, vibrant brands and courageous, positive minds and unravels, in a compelling storytelling style, what makes a brand a survivor when faced with severe adversity."

–PANKAJ SETHI

Former President, Tata Teleservices Ltd.

"Not a day too soon, the book written by Vijay Parthasarathy, an experienced corporate leader himself, opens our eyes to discover the Golden Ladder: the two legs of domain expertise and our limitless mind which together stabilise the uncertainties of every business—small, medium or large—we see in today's business world. ***The book is an instruction manual*** *which teaches us disciplined execution and many best practices, producing tremendous outcomes in scaling one's business. In a series of real-life examples using both Indian and international case studies, Vijay Parthasarathy has unfolded the secrets and intricacies of business success.* **A must-read book** *for both business entrepreneurs and aspiring executives!"*

–KANDASWAMY BHARATHAN

Joint Managing Director, Kavithalaya Productions; Adjunct Faculty IIMA, ISB.

"A book that can transform you and bring out the magical diamond in you. ***A must-read."***

–UNNI WARRIER

Bay Area Serial Entrepreneur, Investor

"What Vijay has set out to do, with success measured over many decades and transitions, is to create a model, the Golden Ladder, that anyone who embarks on a 'Vision Mission' exercise must read and internalise prior to starting the journey. And if you are wondering if this exercise is one only for 'making your company look good', you need to read this now.

"And then we come to those that dream big and who know what to do to get them going on the path to realising their dream but are frustrated that 'today's youngsters' don't see the 'larger picture' and are moving on at short notice just to 'earn an extra buck'. For them, Vijay provides a script that will enable every employee not just to buy into their vision but live and work with them each day of their lives, to take the company where they want it to be!

"In the process, Vijay demonstrates an uncanny ability to speak with (not at) you and embed in you the unwavering belief that you can, once you set on the path, be a legend in and beyond your lifetime.

***RISE TO BE UNSTOPPABLE is an invaluable gift** to dreamer leaders who dream big and engage every sinew of theirs each day of their lives in making their dream a reality!"*

–HARI PADMANABHAN

Chairman,Encore International, Dubai; Serial Investor

*"Vijay Parthasarathy is a man who can see through brands and their impact on society. Having worked with many global names himself, he understands and presents deep and profound concepts; yet they are simple to understand and implement. **I highly recommend this book,** especially for those entrepreneurs and experts who want to build a brand that will stand the test of time."*

–SIDDHARTH RAJSEKAR

Founder, Internet Lifestyle Hub; India's leading Digital Coach,
International best-selling Author

"No one better to talk about how to build a business and a brand than Vijay Parthasarathy. Having known him for long, he brings extraordinary creativity to solving business problems. His training, experience and insights developed over the years will be invaluable to any entrepreneur or executive in making his company a high-performing, sustainable and resilient enterprise. This book draws on the essence of his experience and provides valuable lessons."

–SUDHAKAR KESAVAN

Former Chairman & CEO, ICF Global, USA

ABOUT THE AUTHOR

Vijay Parthasarathy, an alumnus of IIT Kanpur and IIM Ahmedabad and a former global CEO, discovered something fascinating while analysing hundreds of businesses that collapsed during the Covid pandemic. It struck him that these companies were not privy to a specific, powerful science. A science that legends such as Johnson & Johnson, Procter & Gamble, Colgate-Palmolive, Coke, Nike, Apple, Unilever and Tata have understood and mastered. A science that allows them to dominate their industry for centuries, rendering them immune to every kind of adversity that could threaten them. Having been a part of the growth story of most of these legends with experience across 75 brands and having helped elevate a brand from the drawing board as the first employee to over $100 million in global revenue, the author shares that remarkable science in this book. If followed systematically, this science can take your company to levels you never thought possible and keep you atop the mountain of giants.

A science that recognises that in addition to hard work, intelligence, education, technology, experience and competence, ***a unique template*** needs to be followed to shine beyond the ordinary. Only when that template is firmly embedded in the business roadmap will the gates to the world of the exemplary and extraordinary open.

Vijay is also certified in hypnotherapy, Reiki, Art of Living (AOL) and Brahma Kumaris meditation technique. He is a staunch practitioner of Cognitive Behavioural Therapy (CBT), Neuro-linguistic Programming (NLP) and Acceptance and Commitment Therapy (A.C.T). He has successfully used this vast knowledge to overcome severe anxiety disorders and depression. Deeply studying the nuances and intricacies of the ***human mind***, he now finds himself in a place better than ever. In this book, he brings together this revolutionary combination of a unique form of domain expertise and channelling mind power, unlike anyone has done before. A combination which is an absolute must to shine like that eternal 'Diamond in the Sky'!

Vijay can be contacted at mantras@vijayparthasarathy.com

CONTENTS

Dedicated to

To have the faith your son can cross any mountain, when his own thoughts were stumbling, to constantly demonstrate that 'to manifest' was as easy as eating a pie, Dear Nanna, you have been my greatest inspiration and continue to be with me always, though you left early.

Dear Amma, you scripted pain with a smile while constantly rescripting me to believe that I could rise to the greatest heights. That you left me just before this book was released makes me feel certain that you wanted to take your time in heaven to read at leisure while blessing me from the top.

ACKNOWLEDGEMENTS

For going beyond the boundaries of arduous labour and *editing patiently, Mrs Tara Ramkumar, my sincere thanks.*

For ensuring money never loses its glitter by providing all the ingredients for the finance chapter, thank you, my dear friend, Ambarish.

To all the innumerable friends from every walk of life who came forward in support, my immense gratitude. To my dear wife Radha, who relentlessly pushes me to go beyond what I am, my bright, loving daughters, Namisha and Nina (Niharika), my wonderful son-in-law, Raghunath and my twinkle-eyed princess, my granddaughter Ishika, thank you all so much. Thank you for bringing a dimension to my life I thought never existed. The width and depth you bring to all that you do makes me swell with pride.

Nothing can ever be complete without the divine guidance and grace for which I am eternally grateful.

THE GOLDEN LADDER
RISE TO
BE UNSTOPPABLE

21 'SECRET Mantras' to Transform You
Into a Timeless Business Legend

The Game-Changing, Step-by-Step Transformational Guide
to Catapult Your Business and Help You Remain at the Top,
Unlocking the Secret Science of Business Legends

VIJAY PARTHASARATHY

The Momentous Flight...

It was no ordinary Thanksgiving Day. Time would be witness to this day that would soon find a special place in history books. It was late afternoon, with a hint of a drizzle outside. The young man, all of twenty-three, was in a sweat as he pondered for one final moment on the crazy yet life-changing journey he was embarking on. He could not believe he was actually pulling it off. Having dropped out of a lucrative investment banking job after graduating from Stanford, he now found himself suddenly outside the sleepy airport in Portland, Oregon. As the boarding announcement for the flight to Tokyo came crackling through, he knew he couldn't turn back. The year was 1962. The embers of the fires of Hiroshima and Nagasaki had not yet been doused and Japan was not the hottest place for an American to be, let alone for a business proposition. But he knew deep inside he needed to do this. As he stepped inside the aircraft, the captain rattled off the instructions in Japanese, of which he understood nothing and the plane streamed across the sky towards Tokyo. He wondered whether his return ticket would be of any avail or if he would even make it back alive.

But one thing was certain. He was determined to leave a mark. On the planet. One that people would look up to for generations and remind themselves that the man who was the architect of the slogan 'Just Do It', truly lived up to it. Every minute.

That was Phil Knight. The man who brought Nike to the world.

He dared. To dream.

He defied every odd. Challenged all conventional wisdom.

Made people stare at him in disbelief at what he proposed to do. But he did. Only to stand tall and *RISE TO BECOME UNSTOPPABLE*, as the world stood aside to let him enter those coveted gates of immortality and watch with admiration. A legend was born on that eventful day.[1]

He had ascended the Golden Ladder. To become Unstoppable.

...almost fifty years later...

The Wake-Up Call

Bangalore, 6 a.m. A September morning. A distant cuckoo welcomes the transition from twilight. A few other birds join the symphony.

The year is 2011. A beautiful day. Not to be any ordinary one, however. Something happened. I could not get up. A palpable anxiety was gnawing at my chest and I did not even know why. Towards evening it had transformed into a full-blown panic attack.

The days slowly expanded into weeks, the weeks into months and the months continued their stretch into years. I struggled through the bylanes, shuffling between psychotherapists and psychiatrists, all the while in stealth mode to avoid the chance of meeting someone familiar. Of these professionals, some were profound shams and quacks, while others who pretended to be beyond were, in fact, no better. But my wallet saw a dip ranging from Rs. 500 to a whopping Rs. 20,000 per hour every time I left their offices.

Having travelled the distance in my career to quite a high, with material blessings ranging from a sprawling duplex villa in the heart of Bangalore to luxury cars and having my daughters attend the best Ivy League universities in the US, this was a new experience that had me blindsided, as it unfolded totally inexplicably.

While the world saw these material possessions as 'having it all', in those moments, my only craving was to transition from this agonising mental pain into the world of the ordinary.

I was willing to relinquish it all just to feel normal. This trauma which swayed between depression and obsessive-compulsive disorder (OCD) was heading in directions which threatened to throw me into the sea of dysfunctionality.

Having long been reputed to place discipline above everything else for over thirty years, I now found myself unable to stick to a basic routine. There was a time when neither Germany's sub-zero temperatures nor the scorching Dubai deserts were showstoppers for my daily routine of a 45-minute/6-km morning walk and now the simple act of getting out of bed was near impossible. This rigour ensured that my physical parameters were great but insufficient to erase the mental pain at that moment.

Though Covid has now reset many dimensions of perception, as a society we continue to operate in a zone where meeting a psychiatrist does cast shadows and creates social stigmas. We don't recognise that meeting a doctor to alleviate the pain of the mind is as acceptable as seeking help to relieve physical discomfort. The mental anguish had to be therefore dealt with surreptitiously, twisting the knife into the wound.

Then came the day when it was impossible to stay locked in. I had to travel to Mumbai for a critical meeting as the advisor to one of today's hottest start-ups in the multilingual pace, Indus OS (recently acquired by PhonePe, a fintech giant). Still, my anxiety was reaching a breaking point where I could not take one step toward going to the airport. To put things in perspective, I was someone who had travelled the world with seven passports filled with visa stamps from nearly fifty countries. But that day was the exact opposite. The anxiety and fear were killing me. Niharika, my younger daughter, had to accompany me to the airport and, observing my plight, got herself a ticket to fly with me, while my good friend Pankaj Sethi had to take special permission to enter Mumbai airport after we landed to escort me out. How I managed to make it to the meeting and put on a straight face for those two hours is a nightmare that I would rather not recall.

Then, one day, something I had read long ago came flashing at me—the event in 1962 that had reshaped history. About that young twenty-three-year-old Nike genius. Who overcame every obstacle that threatened his very existence, personally and professionally. Who rediscovered a new science that the legends continue to store in their dossiers and the only code that could unlock the mystery of what it takes for someone to shine on top for centuries.

Lying in bed on one of those listless days, recalling this story changed everything.

Here I was with a potentially wonderful future but succumbing to the vagaries of the mind and frittering it away. My dream of working on a significant cause, of creating an ecosystem of powerful entrepreneurs and business leaders, using my domain and professional skills seemed to be fading into the background. It then occurred to me that if I were to somehow transcend these mental roadblocks, I would then have a potion which would effectively combine my field of business expertise along with *yet another factor* in a unique manner. A formula used by all the celebrated organisations and individuals to achieve the feat of fame and endurance. A recipe that could create timeless icons making a visible difference to themselves, their organisations and their country.

It suddenly was very clear.

I had to do it. I had to get back onto the ship I had slipped from into those stormy seas. I had to ascend what I called The Golden Ladder.

Crossing the Red Ocean of Despair

The immediate step I embarked on was to do everything possible to overcome this mental turmoil. Being a certified practitioner of Reiki (an ancient energy healing technique), Art of Living & Brahma Kumaris meditation practices and hypnotherapy, with mastery of CBT, the powerful Acceptance and Commitment Therapy (A.C.T) and the hundreds of books that have guided me over the years, I slowly rebuilt all that was missing, thus carefully crossing this ocean of despair into the safe shores of tranquillity. And even sanity. **I was now at a place with far more power and energy than I ever was before.**

I believed I now had the right ingredients to make my dream come alive.

So, why this story?

This parable takes credence because a relentless pursuit of *domain excellence* in the world envelops us, mostly with *flawed models.* With a fabric that deceives us into the belief that nothing else matters. Here I was, with the very best of credentials, from an IIT and IIM Ahmedabad, as well as a successful, global CEO enjoying all the fruits that typically accompany such a title. If the above could happen to me and without much warning or knowledge, there must be something in addition to all that which would be yet another 'necessary' and 'special' condition for someone to truly shine.

If this condition were also overlaid with a unique business excellence blueprint followed by the legends, unlike the flawed one mistakenly chased by the majority, there would emerge the 'perfect recipe'. A special potion to create something extraordinary that will live beyond the physical realm and ensure you leave a timeless stamp on the planet.

This journey is an exploration of that world.

HOW THIS BOOK CAN WORK MIRACLES FOR YOU

And Unlock the Secret of Your Magical Goose

> *"The cowards never started. The weak died along the way. And that leaves us" –Phil Knight, Shoe Dog*

The proverbial magical goose. The one that lays golden eggs every day. What if a mantra existed that could bring the riches of the enchanted goose into your life? Through a start-up you are embarking on, a business that has been around for a few years but is just limping along. A mantra that could guide you seamlessly to create the next legendary company akin to Nike or Apple. Also create in you the special strength to retain the eggs and resist the temptation of cutting open the goose!

This book is precisely that *mantra*. Not one, but a formidable set of many. Mantras that create not just 'also ran' entities, but legends, as I like to refer to them. Individuals and companies that have traversed decades, created a legacy and continued to live beyond their time.

They are the ones who have *not* crumbled with just one pandemic, Covid, but have withstood the onslaught of both the World Wars, the Spanish Flu, the Great Depression, the Bubonic Plague and many other pandemics along the way. Not just *withstood* but have been at the absolute pinnacle, never letting go of the No.1 slot for centuries. They remain legends even in 2023. And sometimes selling just ordinary products. So, what do they know that seems to be eluding all others? This book unravels that secret science I have had the privilege to witness through my own experiences.

This book is for you if you have a deep, insatiable hunger and passion for becoming a legend in whichever field you choose. Someone who leaves the kind of legacy the world talks about for centuries beyond their physical existence. It's for those of you who will leave the Earth knowing you have made an indelible difference.

This book outlines the cardinal principles that have made companies such as Procter & Gamble, Colgate-Palmolive, Nike, Johnson & Johnson, Coke, Tata and Apple reign over the world. It sets the specific mantras for each of these 'principles' which prompt the wonder goose to work its magic and lay its golden eggs.

A Few Pointers for This Journey

This book is not merely a vehicle for scaling up your business by a paltry twenty or thirty per cent. It is not even an avenue for revving up from 80 kmph to 100 kmph or even 160 kmph. This book is about entirely rescripting your modality. It is about changing to a radical transportation mode, shifting to an aircraft paradigm, allowing you to breeze at 800 kmph or higher. It's about creating a quantum shift in perspective and orientation to help you vibrate at a totally new frequency.

You need to filter the essence from everything said here, apply it to wherever you are and project it onto where you would like to see yourself. It has nothing to do with any limitations that your mind may throw at you, either in terms of relevance or achievability or even questioning your ability, with words of fear cloaked as practicality. You will then witness the legend emerge from within you.

What This Book Is Not

This book is not a GRQS (Get Rich Quick Scheme). This is *not* about cutting and killing the magical goose to remove all the eggs at once. There were none, remember? Greed never took anyone far.

This book is also not about doing some '*jugaad*' to uncannily beat the system and cut short the arduous journey undertaken by the legends.

Neither is it a recipe to replicate the products or services that others have done.

It is for that special one driven by the desire to be immortal.

It is a manual for transformation from the ordinary to the legendary.

For those who aspire to *stand apart* from the crowd and smile, knowing a job has been well done, as the world watches in

admiration. If systematically followed with patience and faith, ***nothing can stop you.***
Most references and examples in the book are from first-hand experiences as I witnessed them unfolding before my eyes.

It is my strong conviction that no amount of research, either desk or conversational, can match the validity and intensity of what someone witnesses personally. Hence, while there could be other organisations which match up to the qualities this book alludes to, I have chosen to focus more on legends of whom I've had the privilege and good fortune of getting a ringside view.

One Final Word

While this book aims to create and unleash that legend in you and to script the business of the century, you can use it with equal efficacy to achieve many of life's other purposes, including excellent health and intimate relationships. It would, of course, help if you donned a different cloak for each of those, as you will witness in the unfolding of this book.

Welcome then, to the Land of Miracles! With one difference.
YOU will *create* each miracle. So, get ready to take on this journey with me and take a place among the legendary giants.

PART ONE

MANTRAS TO POWER THE FIRST (LEFT) LEG

MANTRA 1

THE GOLDEN LADDER

The Maha Mantra

> *Entrepreneurship is fervently climbing the ladder of success. 'Legendariness' is ensuring the ladder is perfectly anchored on both the legs.*

Often, we see many individuals and companies who do 'seemingly' well. Yes, they generate revenues and even profits (*yes, in an era dominated by valuation, which may not have a relationship to profits, this does sound like an anachronism*) and show off employees and offices and life seems okay. Yes, just 'okay.'

On the other hand, a select few, be it Steve Jobs, William Procter & James Gamble (P&G), Elon Musk, the Johnson brothers of J&J, Bill Gates, Jeff Bezos, Phil Knight, Ratan Tata, Mukesh Ambani, Narayana Murthy, Azim Premji or a few others, seem to vibrate at an entirely different, elevated frequency. Where things seem to happen effortlessly and whatever they do seems to have that famous 'Midas touch'. What is it that they do that is so different?

Unveiling the ***FIRST*** *and the* ***Maha Mantra*** *in this journey of the Unstoppables:*

After studying most of these legends in various ways, I have understood that these people have ascended what I refer to as the **Golden Ladder,** the ladder that is beyond the reach of the general milieu but the coveted possession of only a few. The ladder that is not visible to the naked eye but can be observed only through a special lens. The ladder that will help you rise sky-high.

So, what is this Golden Ladder?

Like any ladder, this, too, stands on two legs. But in this instance, the two legs are unique. Not being aware of this uniqueness and sometimes, even after being cognizant, the inability to leverage its distinctiveness is the sole reason for many to be at the bottom of this great ladder. The place at the bottom that leaves many gasping, with the rhetorical question of what makes the ascent so uncommon, where mere hard work and intelligence alone are not the building blocks for its rungs.

The answer lies essentially in our ability to spot one vital factor, the one that sets the legends apart. The one that is constantly staring us in the face but seems to be escaping our attention.

It is the ability to bring both legs of the ladder into focus rather than be oblivious to one or the other.

Ironically, the bitter truth is that most individuals power and firmly anchor only one leg of this ladder while completely

neglecting the other. They thus remain at the bottom of the Golden Ladder, with the top always being a distant dream.
But the legends who shine up there know the magic of *powering and anchoring* **both** the legs. As a result, it's no surprise that they inspire admiration.

What exactly are these two legs?

The most focused First Leg (the Left Leg)
This leg is the zone where the majority work themselves to death. Night and day, immersing themselves in objectives, deadlines, targets, acquisitions, revenues, travel, along with the madness around everything that seemingly gets them to the end of the rainbow. But rarely does. *Following a business model which could be completely flawed.* A model devoid of a few 'secret ingredients' critical to business dominance. Known only to a select few but escape the majority. Let us call this the ***domain leg***.

This is the place where each, as per their passion and competence, enters and generates that incredible output, most of the time outshining a million others, only to be surpassed by someone at some point in the future. Sheerly due to the ignorance of this *'secret knowledge'*.

The untouched & often neglected Second Leg (the Right Leg)
This Right Leg is the one that few dare to touch. Not due to fear but being ignorant of its potency and power.
The leg that differentiates between the great and the invincible.
The leg that comes with no instruction manual on how to power

or anchor it. But one that is a million times more powerful than the Left Leg.
This Right Leg, therefore, is the one that can elevate you to the heights of success or lower you to the depths of despair.

While people fallaciously believe their success is due to the labour of the **Left Leg** alone, the sole reason the legends are insurmountable in their ventures lies elsewhere. It is because, knowingly or unknowingly, they have also been able to anchor and power the **Right Leg** while fine-tuning certain elements of the **Left Leg** with a *unique formula.*
This **Right Leg** is also known as *THE MIND.*

To be up there, to shine brighter than the ordinary, requires us to have both the legs powered and firmly entrenched in a solid foundation. This entrenchment provides us with the incredible strength to start the upward climb on this Golden Ladder. Only in the success of this ascent will we find the magical goose waiting to lay the 'golden eggs'.

This book is the manual on how **YOU, too**, can master the 'powering' of both the legs of this Golden Ladder and set out on the journey to the esoteric place at the top.

MANTRA 2

FAR AWAY ON THE DISTANT HORIZON

Setting a Legendary Vision

VISION, MISSION, VALUES

"

The only advantage of not knowing where you are heading is that you don't have to worry about being lost.

The year: 1984. Month: November. Around 250 people had gathered in one of the prestigious five-star hotels of Mumbai (erstwhile Bombay). A closed-door, three-day event. As a fresh marketing manager at Johnson & Johnson, I was kindled with curiosity and anticipation regarding this annual event where newcomers were not privy to the agenda. I soon realised this was not a conference to discuss mundane revenue and profitability targets. Nor was it a motivational seminar to power-launch the new set of CEOs into the world.

This gathering was different. One could feel it in the air.

As the Managing Director walked in and set the theme in motion, I could not believe my ears.
WHAT? They would spend the next three days discussing one single subject? And that too, from my beginner's perspective, a topic that had no direct impact on the business at hand? Just the vision, mission and values of the company? Was it worth all this effort, time and money?
How wrong and short-sighted I was!

The next three days were a voyage through the incredible. Never in my wildest dreams could I have pictured someone dwelling on this theme with such intensity. A subject which until then assumed only minor importance in my mind was now taking centre-stage!

That day, I understood the most important reason why some were enshrined in the Hall of Legends. It was my eureka moment of recognising the criticality of the life-changing tenets of these giants.

This all-powerful MANTRA was made up of a clear sight of the vision, purpose, mission and values of the organisation.

This clarity is what sets them apart. Only when these are in place can anyone dare to dream of being the diamond that shines so brightly in the sky.

This exercise of ingraining the essence of 'Our Credo' in its employees is the holiest activity that Johnson & Johnson sets great store by.

'Our Credo', is what Johnson & Johnson lives by, honestly believes is its most robust purpose, its raison d'être, its commitment to itself and the world.

The organisation's vision, mission and values have been set in stone since 1886, 137 years ago. And each year across the globe, over 250 people in every country it operates in meet to infuse themselves with the values, imbibe every element, ingest every letter, discuss, brainstorm, clear their minds of the cobwebs and align with the vision and mission.

The company is unequivocal when it says about its credo, "The fact that Johnson & Johnson is one of only a handful of companies that have flourished through more than a century of change is evidence of that." *-jjvision.com*

Why do they have to do this?

If you honestly believe in where you want to reach, have the intense desire to make it happen and reflect on who you indeed are, then no force in the Universe can stop you.

That is precisely why they do this.

The reason why it is a celebrated institution. Even in 2023, Johnson & Johnson has been named '*Fortune* World's Most Admired Company' and ranked #1 on the Pharmaceutical Industry List[1].

After 137 years, it has remained steadfast in the enviable number one position, having overcome multiple crises.

Amidst the reign of today's giants such as Amazon, Google, Facebook and Microsoft, here is an interesting observation. Every legend we discuss in this book, those privy to the secret sauce that bestows glory, has been on this planet longer than most, if not all, of these modern tech mammoths *put together.*

Vision is the strongest reason for this achievement. The clear mission, the step-by-step manual and the unassailable values which form the core and essence of who we are, shape and open the conduit towards this endeavour.

Vision is what you see for thousands of miles if you stand on the highest mountain, beyond what the ordinary on Earth can. In the epic *Ramayana*, Hanuman stands atop the Mahendragiri Parvat (the highest mountain in that range) and acquires the vision of where he must go, only a theoretical feat for all the monkey soldiers at the bottom. However, this vision propelled his journey and the genesis of his eventual victory.

The one without vision will soon be groping for eyesight.

WHAT ARE VISION, MISSION and VALUES?

Many often confuse vision and mission, to start with. What exactly is a Vision Statement and how do you create one?

1. A Vision Statement is that large grand goal (LGG), a picture you see clearly in a faraway time.
2. A picture that is *not* about you.
3. It is *not* about revenue or profit numbers' metrics.
4. It is about what *you* do *for others* that will define you and thereby bring you ecstasy.

5. It is about that which makes a holistic, global impact and lives beyond the one who created it.
6. It is about the emotional enrichment you bring to the audience you cater to by solving their most profound physical and other challenges.

Here are some examples of the most extraordinary vision statements.

NIKE

"To bring inspiration and innovation to every athlete in the world."[2]

Regarded as the last word in legend creation, Nike is the epitome of how important a company's vision is and even more so, how it is painstakingly executed. Nike's vision stems from the core of how it sees the future of sport in a holistic manner. In this, it creates a transformational arena for itself and the world, an admirable act in every way.

Nike does not make shoes.
It creates geniuses in sport.
Legends in the arena of athletics.

APPLE

"To make the best products on Earth and to leave the world better than we found it."[3]

To say this company has transformed the world is to undermine its power a million times. What Apple has achieved is not just revolutionary or legendary but awe-inspiring! Steve Jobs in 1987 had said, *"The people who are crazy enough to think they can change the world are probably the ones who do.*" That was his vision. To change the world. And he did. This thinking is the hallmark of legends who ensure their footprints are printed on the planet, even if they were small.

JOHNSON & JOHNSON

A company that has withstood the test of time has its vision as the barometer for any Johnsonian's existence and purpose within the organisation.

'OUR CREDO' -Johnson & Johnson

"We believe our first responsibility is to the patients, doctors and nurses, to mothers and fathers and all others who use our products and services. In meeting their needs, everything we do must be of high quality. We must constantly strive to provide value, reduce costs and maintain reasonable prices. Customers' orders must be serviced promptly and accurately.

Our business partners must have an opportunity to make a fair profit.

"We are responsible to our employees who work with us throughout the world. We must provide an inclusive work environment where each person must be considered an individual. We must respect their diversity and dignity and recognise their merit. They must have a sense of security, fulfilment and purpose in their jobs. Compensation must be fair and adequate and working conditions, clean, orderly and safe. We must support the health and well-being of our employees and help them fulfil their family and other personal responsibilities. Employees must feel

free to make suggestions and complaints. There must be equal employment, development and advancement opportunities for those qualified. We must provide competent leaders whose actions must be just and ethical.

"We are responsible to the communities in which we live and work and to the world community. We must help people be healthier by supporting better access and care in more places worldwide. We must be good citizens — support good works and charities, better health and education and bear our fair share of taxes. We must maintain the property we are privileged to use in good order, protecting the environment and natural resources.

"Our final responsibility is to our stockholders. Businesses must make a sound profit. We must experiment with new ideas. Research must be carried on, innovative programs developed, investments made for the future and mistakes paid for. New equipment must be purchased, new facilities provided and new products launched. Reserves must be created to provide for adverse times. When operating according to these principles, the stockholders should realise a fair return."[4]

WALT DISNEY

"To be one of the world's leading producers and providers of entertainment and information."[5]

Yet another company that stands tall for its vision. It is how it sees itself from atop that glass tower, a thousand feet up in the sky, towards a million miles ahead in the future. In terms of the world market, it is focused on what and whom it serves to command a dominant leadership position.

COLGATE-PALMOLIVE

"We are Colgate, a caring, innovative growth company that is reimagining a future for all the people, their pets and the planet."[6]
A statement that sees into a future not many can. As I mentioned earlier, a statement about *what you do for others* at a holistic level is what defines you.

This is a company selling seemingly ordinary products that can be manufactured by many, the likes of toothpaste and toothpowder. However, it has been able to withstand and sustain any aggression, environmental or political or competition, for 216 years, all while remaining number one in its business. Boy, it needs to be placed on a pedestal and worshipped for its achievements! That is Colgate-Palmolive. Colgate describes its care for humanity, the animal kingdom and the whole planet in every act. Yes, it is grandiose, but that constitutes a vision, a purpose that inspires everyone to achieve it when painted on a canvas of sincerity.

PROCTER & GAMBLE

"Be and be recognised as, the best consumer products and services company in the world"[7]

Beginning with fourteen employees 136 years ago, P&G stands tall in everything it does, whether mundane or transformational products. Not without reason.

It incorporates how it defines itself 'to be' the best and also be recognised as such in every business segment they represent.

GOOGLE

"To provide access to the world's information in one click."[8]

This philosophy succinctly captures its outlook and intentions to contribute to the world's wellbeing.

Finally, a peek into India's highest-valued brand

TATA

"To be globally significant in each of our chosen businesses by 2025."[9]

To be in line with the best. This is exactly what rings loud from their vision statement.Tata has made a holistic and all-encompassing vision to make a significant difference globally. Here the TATA Group has set a definite timeline, unlike a few others.

Having set the path for the future as they see it, let us take a closer look at mission statements.

What constitutes the mission of an organisation?

The vision you have seen from atop the mountain requires distinct processes and steps to execute.

It needs specific principles to be followed. There will be definite challenges to overcome and clear, precise solutions to surmount those challenges to make the vision a reality.

This detailing is the spine of the mission statement.

Every small and big step you take to reach that coveted place you have seen in your vision constitutes your Mission Statement.

It could be

1. Products and services you plan to focus on
2. The technology you propose to deploy to make that possible

3. People, the skills and the attitudes you will inculcate in them

In a more simplistic sense, if your vision is to head from Bangalore to that small lake in the hills of Darjeeling (a hill station in east India), then all the steps that constitute reaching there would define the mission. Be it the taxi ride to the airport, the airline that you would choose to transport you there, the hotels that make your stay memorable, as well as the multitude of details that need to be factored in, to make your journey from point A (Bangalore) to point B (the lake in Darjeeling) possible.

Here are some great examples of mission:

NIKE
"Do everything possible to expand human potential. We do that by creating ground-breaking sport innovations, by making our products more sustainable, by building a creative and diverse global team and by making a positive impact in communities where we live and work."[10]

APPLE
"To bring the best user experience to customers through innovative hardware, software and services."[11]

GOOGLE
"Organize the world's information and make it universally accessible and useful."[12]

It is evident. It is what the organisation would do at every step of its journey to make the vision possible. From the minor detail to the most significant stride, it permeates every element and aspect of what it does to be in complete synchrony with the vision and purpose.

PROCTER & GAMBLE

"We will provide branded products and services of superior quality and value that improve the lives of the world's consumers now and for generations to come."[13]

Specifics on the kind of products, services and quality levels along with the duration they would achieve it in is what this mission statement beautifully carves out. With a time horizon that matches its vision.

TATA

"To be the most reliable global network for customers and suppliers, that delivers value through products and services. To be a responsible value creator for all our stakeholders."[14]

It has, in no uncertain terms, defined its path – through its products, services and the all-important aspect of the entire stakeholder community. The key word being 'reliable'.

The above vision and mission statements would just be a set of feel-good words in English if they did not have one basic attribute: A foundation that ensures adherence and continuity with the rigour of an army drill, an almost fanatic, obsessive philosophical base that guarantees not just their continuance but sets their path ablaze for those who rigorously follow it.

And that foundation is *the values* all these greats hold on to resolutely.

Values are the wall against which the Golden Ladder leans.
Seemingly obvious but not quite.
There is a choice.
If they were listed with simply the objective of 'sounding good,' they would not stand the test of time or even enter the framework of our discussion.
These are the nerve endings, the sinews of the people. When you wake them up in the middle of the night and threaten them with even the direst consequences, they would hold these principles dearer than their lives.
Their values are not just cast in stone. They are integrated into their DNA.

Here are a few notable examples:

COLGATE-PALMOLIVE
"Caring, Global Teamwork, Continuous Improvement."[15]

GOOGLE
"Protecting users, expanding opportunity, including all voices, responding to crises, advancing sustainability."[16]

TATA
"Pioneering
Integrity
Excellence
Unity
Responsibility"[17]
As is amply evident, these powerful tenets have kept brand Tata at that enviable No.1 position in India for over a hundred years.

PROCTER & GAMBLE

"Integrity
Leadership
Ownership
Passion for winning
Trust"[18]

Trust and ownership define the company's core beliefs which have long-lasting effects on its stakeholders. At the same time, passion for winning constitutes their attitude to perfection.

APPLE

"Accessibility
Support education
A planet-sized plan
We're all in
Privacy is a human right
Racial equity and justice"[19]

NIKE

"Community
Sustainability
Diversity
Social responsibility"[20]

All these values are beyond the fundamentals of honesty, integrity and hard work. Those have not taken their place of honour here because they are taken for granted. Honesty, integrity and hard work are the foundational core devoid of which we do not dare say we have a journey. Like Jack Welch

says, *"Integrity is just a ticket to the game. If you don't have it, you shouldn't even be allowed onto the field."*
Of course, there is no harm if one wants to reiterate these as P&G does.

My favourite value is Empathy.
When we have empathy as a value, we can instantly view the situation from the other's standpoint without either negating or challenging it. A state of mind that keeps your emotion in 'pause mode' while analysing the path to a solution. Each time. In a nutshell, empathy alone can take care of most situations that create a divide between the customer and the company.
Not a day passes without one witnessing companies that suddenly veer off the track into oblivion. For the discerning, the reason is apparent: A state of mismatch between their vision, mission and values.
Arthur Andersen, one of the top accounting firms, found itself in a downward spiral when its eagerness to grow at an unsustainable pace made it embrace consulting, a business that was not very aligned to its existing practices. The single reason is the discord between mission and values.[21]
Similarly, Enron is a perfect example of being at the receiving end of embarking on a peripheral trading business versus focusing on its core business of pipeline and energy. Once again, a conflict between mission/vision and values.[22] Thus, in summary, *while vision makes you see beyond what everyone does and create a Mad Audacious Dream (MAD), mission outlines every individual step you need to take to accomplish that vision.*

To reiterate, these include products or services that you provide, technology and learnings that you and your team imbibe and the quality and genre of people you carry along on your journey. Values are those powerfully steadfast beacons which constantly remind you whether your voyage is on the right course. This is the wall against which the Golden Ladder leans.

The VMV Transference

One afternoon at work many years ago, I was entering the lunchroom with the MD. We were still ecstatic about creating an exceptional vision, mission and values (VMV) statement. We designed beautiful neck badges for employees, spelling out this philosophy vividly. Life seemed hunky-dory and we were convinced of its blossoming.

But as we came down the stairs, something took me by complete surprise, almost a shock.

The VP (Manufacturing) and the VP (Operations), seated at a table below, hurriedly picked up the neck badge that was casually strewn across the lunch table and put it around their necks.

I just could not believe my eyes. What we regarded as holy, other senior members viewed as a chore, as though they only wore it out of fear of being reprimanded. God! It then struck me.

This vision and mission were mine and that of the MD. Period. It stopped there.

It was not a vision that was shared by everyone else. It was suddenly as clear as the sky the previous night. There was no way this vision would be achieved.

Only the two of us believed in it. The rest were unaware or had no reason to believe in it.
Any boat with only two rowing would not get far.

The lesson that presented itself that day was startlingly clear. Every vision must be shared *a*nd each employee should buy into the ownership if that vision were to see the light of day.

The lesson herein, therefore, is to: Ensure you have your vision clearly outlined and that the entire organisation buys into it and the mission in all its specificity scripted and suffused with the values you will die for and uphold under the direst of circumstances. Now you have a head start to the league of the legends, far away from the madding crowd of also-rans.

When there is a shared vision, you don't need supervision.

This process of involvement, in essence, is the summary. When the founder's vision penetrates everyone, a deep sense of ownership surges to the surface within each person leading to a passion that transmutes every obstacle into a challenge to be embraced.
How, therefore, to create this shared vision?

1. The Vision Meeting
   A coming together of all the stakeholders of your company where you present the vision, followed by a painstaking brainstorming of all its elements, possibilities, challenges and virtues.
   Remember, at the end of the day, it is YOUR vision. It is your company. What you are attempting through this exercise is

a fine-tuning, with its edges smoothed and people's thoughts aligned with yours so that it becomes a collective dream.

But it is also possible that some may not share this vision and may have a diametrically opposite view.

It does not mean that your vision is incorrect or that you need to change it as per others.

It just means that they are not aligned with it.

So, the choice lies between setting a time frame for the alignment of views or engaging in the challenging task of letting them go if they are too wide of the mark.

When you have absolute conviction about your vision and that energy shows, it brings people who tune into that frequency. Thus, when you seek people to work on your team, you will attract those who believe in your vision. They then would not work just for the pay packet at the end of the month because it is their personal dream they are chasing now. Even into the wee hours of the night. Even when no one is watching. They will be there whenever anything matters.

2. Incorporating Others' Inputs

   Inasmuch as you do not change your vision, it is vital that the team's inputs are incorporated to achieve effective collaboration in the vision. You will be amazed at how people produce fascinating recommendations when their inputs are valued.

   These would help generate focus, eliminate duplication, clear the haze in the glass and make the destination far more visible while keeping the overall vision intact.

Once again, while you incorporate inputs from everyone, remember, the vision is finally YOURS.

3. Periodic Review

   A critical element Johnson & Johnson has drilled into my DNA. This is the master key to ensuring success. Many a book has been written about how we set the most grandiose goals only to remember a year later that they still need to be achieved.

   A review meeting, preferably once a quarter, is a definite must to guarantee the success of the vision. The course, its achievement and the challenges in its journey are a few key elements that should go into this review.

   These review meetings must necessarily be open to discussing and debating every suggestion made by any team member before taking a call to incorporate or reject them based on their positive or negative impact on the stated and adopted vision statement.

While the mission will find itself embedded in the objectives set for the various parameters, make sure that the values are adhered to since even a slight slacking off will have a tumultuous effect on the vision and derail its success quotient.

You must recognise that your mission may demand various course corrections in managing products, services and other parameters. These changes need to be reflected in the many monthly and other domain-based review meetings that, individually and collectively, the team members would have with or without you.

Do This ACTION Exercise Now!
Write down the most succinct version of the vision you envisage for your company, the mission avenues that you will undertake towards the consummation of that vision, the values that define you and for the sake of which you would stake your life.

You now have a choice.

You can overlook this Mantra as something mundane, like a few may have. If you look around, those are the very people who either fall by the wayside in their journey towards being a legend or are, at best, struggling on a treadmill of perpetual effort and unable to get off, either to smell the roses or to taste the fruit they have been nurturing.

Or you can:

Recognise its holiness and embrace it with all the seriousness as every legend has. The select few who have grasped the enormous significance and sanctity of this Mantra have internalised it through assiduous practice and ensured it flowed in every drop of blood in their veins.

What better reason than that for their legendary status?

MANTRA 3

THE SEARCH FOR THAT ELUSIVE PROBLEM

Decoding the Customer Problem That Truly Matters

> *"Too often we give our children answers to remember than problems to solve." -Roger Lewin.*

It was a Friday afternoon on a sweltering day in Bangalore. I saw my house help hurriedly coming onto the street as I was returning from work early, giving me a great fright. He was supposed to be at home with our bundle of love, Arya, an adorable puppy all of two years. But what was he doing outside and that too alone?

As I approached him, he seemed a little nervous too. When I asked him what exactly happened, with a sullen face he said that he had gotten locked out of the house by accident and did not have the key to get back in. "And Arya?" I asked.

She was inside. My heart sank as we rushed home.

I heaved a huge sigh of relief as I saw Arya inside from the terrace through the mesh door. But the problem remained. How does Arya get out or we get in?

The spare set of keys was with my daughter Namisha, who was quite far, en route to a hill station on a weekend trip. That was almost two hours away, with very little chance of her coming all the way back if she wanted to pursue her journey.

It was unthinkable to leave Arya alone for close to four hours if I had to fetch the keys, even if my daughter were to hold on for two hours till I reached.

I called her. To my great surprise, she stayed calm and said, "Not to worry, Arya will be fine. I will have the keys Dunzoed."

I had no idea what she meant.

But within an hour, I received the keys! Thus, achieving two critical objectives.

a) Not leaving the place I needed to be in, and

b) Saving a few hours of stressful driving in the chaos of Bangalore traffic.

Dunzo is a platform that recognised the existence of such a customer 'problem' and created an army of delivery boys who would be available through an '*app*' to do just this.

Deliver any product from any place to any place quickly.

So, the next MANTRA to reach the Land of the Legends is the ability to 'identify a clear and specific customer problem'.

Here the options run along three lines.

Option 1: Identify a problem no one has solved before

Precisely, this route is what **DUNZO** followed. They recognised the agony of a hundred others like me who would want an article, an urgent letter or a critical medicine to be transported to someone and would go through the same trauma I had gone through. These situations were a 'bulb-on' moment for Dunzo, creating a unique delivery service with the courier boys waiting at different corners of the city to alleviate this problem, turning the venture into an overnight success.

This example, by far, would be the easiest success recipe. The ability to identify a problem many have faced but could not solve or have ignored lends itself to opening the gateway to continued success.

Apple's iPhone is a great example wherein the entire complex user experience landscape of all the phone users was resolved in a single go.

Unlike Dunzo, whose solution was simple and straightforward, Apple spent years researching consumer behaviour, ergonomic biases and scores of areas where the user experience had to be amended. This understanding called for innovation like no other and finally, when it did, the product stormed the market. APPLE was the combination of identifying an exceptionally complex problem and creating an outstandingly creative user experience by employing thousands of geniuses to achieve a seemingly unimaginable solution. This dedication is, of course, what makes it legendary.

Yet another is the success of **SPOTIFY.** While studying the online music market, Ek, the founder, instantly identified a vast vacuum. He realised there was a significant opportunity in the gap between the pirated music of Napster and the overly expensive music of Apple iTunes.

Addressing that gap could be a huge game-changer.

Pirated music came with the baggage of low-quality output and extremely high download times.

That is when **Spotify** hit upon providing value at both ends of the music spectrum for the label owners and the end users. Taking the sting out of downloads, it created a service providing amazingly high-quality and high-speed downloadable 'streaming' music and compensated the labels liberally.

This initiative enhanced the user experience so significantly that the customer was more than happy to pay for streaming, even overlooking other sites offering free downloads.

While this is the most robust route to creating history, it is anything but simple or easy to arrive at such an innovation, requiring a precise understanding of the behavioural patterns of customers.

The Lesson in the making

i) Search for the existence of any '*deep problem*' that has a far-reaching effect on someone in terms of cost, time, effort, health, relationships and entertainment.
ii) Analyse the size of the audience subject to this discomfort.
iii) Assess how big a pain your solution will address and eliminate from the current problem.

If it can reduce the problem by over ninety per cent and the affected audience is sizeable, you have a great start.

Of course, there have been the examples of MakeMyTrip.com or Booking.com where the difficulty of sifting through multiple customer options was resolved through consolidation. Others such as Ola solved the problem of irregular and unorganised taxi systems with 'anywhere, anytime convenience.' The fact that they still have gaping holes in their offering is an opportunity in itself for someone to take on.

Option 2: Evolve a solution for an already identified problem with newer/better solutions

Option 1 may not necessarily be an easy reality, but that does not preclude one from striving to reach the top of the Golden Ladder. Very often, when one finds a large-sized audience in a market led by multiple players, the temptation to carve out a small piece is enormous. But the process of how this is done separates the 'just-revenue-earners' from legends. Entering this large yet scattered market and standing out from the crowd poses unique challenges but is highly possible.

In this scenario, while the first-mover advantage cannot be ignored, if one decides to take a leap of faith and penetrate this competition-entrenched market, it should be based on a simple yet unique *'Power of Three' Formula.*

The Unique 'Power of Three' Formula

My flight was scheduled to depart in 90 minutes and I needed at least thirty, if not forty-five, minutes of drive time to the airport. My taxi was to reach in two minutes. As I awaited its arrival with the eagerness of an expectant father outside the delivery room, I received the (in)famous message, "Your driver has cancelled the trip". My heart sank. It was 5 a.m. and I scrambled to the end of the street, jumped into the first cab that came by and made it to the airport like I was in a Tesla space jet, only to miss the flight! It was a nightmare not worth recounting.

Why, then, does this saga of customer agony continue unabated and what makes yet another brand unable to take on this territory of app-based taxi service is a question many seek without an answer.

Here is the key to this.
It all comes to the *'Power of Three'* test. And the test goes like this.

If a market is fully saturated, a maximum of three brands will likely have the lion's share of the market. Be it Levi's, Lee or Wrangler in jeans, MakeMyTrip, Cleartrip or EaseMyTrip in the travel arena, Nike, Reebok and Adidas in shoes, Coke, Pepsi and Thums Up in soft drinks or Rolex and Omega in watches, it is true of several categories that operate within this sphere. If three brands rule the roost in any segment, it will be a monumental effort to enter that category and almost impossible to make a dent, let alone carve out a place as a legend. On the contrary, if there are less than three major brands in any category, that would be the perfect place to enter and provide solutions to address the existing 'offering gaps' of the current brands.

But, if you truly desire to be legendary, even in a crowded market where battles are fought by many, the MANTRA in the following chapter opens the doors to a science that only a privileged few have been exposed to. A secret science that can make success, even in a three-brand-market, a possibility for the few who exhibit the courage to brave those stormy seas and emerge victorious.

Option 3: Where one 'creates' problems.

This is an arena I would not advocate under any circumstance, but it would be unwise to skip it without mention. An avenue where businesses are created, primarily unimportant ones, but enhanced in their appeal only by way of misinformation or manipulation or a combination of both. Examples range along the avenues of 'how one would be less attractive and be shunned by society if they did not use a specific product' or 'how one would succumb to some disease if they did not follow their sanctified diet product plan'. And the list goes on.

Yes, there has been many a success in this zone. Still, I believe that this manipulation of the vulnerable is outside my value system, which is to provide genuine value and visibly enhance the overall well-being of a customer's physical, mental or emotional space. Hence further discussion of the Option 3 route does not find a place in this book.

In summary, the path to the esoteric zone of legends is through identifying an undiscovered problem that affects a large section of the market and finding a solution to it. Miraculous results await!

One of the methods is to be keenly, consciously and constantly open to everyday activities and be wholly present in any situation that stokes your curiosity or identify a problem that can cause erosion in time and cost or calls for enormous effort. This observation could be a great starting point.

For example, you are driving with your spouse to a party in a crowded arena and irritation chafes at you as time ticks away while you hunt for the ever-elusive parking slot. Can there be a solution whereby, irrespective of your destination, not just malls and hotels, the place has the facility of a valet driver? Someone who is always on standby and who will, within minutes, park your car safely and fetch it when you return?

Or can there be a solution to the problem of an ambulance racing against time with anxious people inside being unable to negotiate the traffic?

Along these lines begins the thinking of the legendary.

Do This ACTION Exercise Now!

What exact problem are you solving for your customer today? Which option category does it fall into? If you have one, does the solution fit the parameters that exemplify a legend? Take time and invest in this before you move on to the all-important mantra.

Let it not be a cause for concern if such solutions are not at the top of your mind or not forthcoming even after rigorous digging into the deepest corners of your mind.

You may be in a business with hundreds of competitors where customers don't seem to stay but shift at the first available additional feature. Or worse, they fall prey to short-term gimmicks and demote themselves to the five-letter word, price. But if you still desire to stand out from the crowd and be legendary, you then are holding in your hands the key to making this masterpiece happen.

MANTRA 4

WHAT BUSINESS ARE YOU REALLY IN?

What You Do Is Not Your 'Real' Business

> *When you buy a watch to notice the time, you have bought a product. When you buy a watch 'to be noticed,' you have bought into a legend.*

This one MANTRA alone, if you imbibe, will elevate your business to unreachable heights. And make you UNSTOPPABLE.

As the cool breeze was blowing on a lazy evening in Bangalore, I decided to walk into one of the most prestigious malls of the city and chanced upon this glitzy store and soon found my feet had followed my eyes. As I sauntered around, I suddenly heard a compelling voice behind me, "Sir, how can I help you?" I turned around to be accosted by a bored, burly man condescendingly looking down at me.

I took hold of myself and asked if they had a particular variant of the product I was looking for.

He asked me, "Sir, is it full steel or half steel-half gold?" I said, "Half steel-half gold."

He said, "Sir, that is sold out for a year."

"How about full steel?"

"Sir, that's sold out for three years."

Then I asked him, "How about full gold?"

He disbelievingly looked at me again and said, "Sir, that's sold out for six months."

I almost blurted out, "In that case, what the hell are you doing here?" But my brain worked better this time as I resisted that temptation.

The variant I was looking for was DAYTONA. And the store: ROLEX.

Consider the best-selling local watch in any country. Even that needs to be sold to over 100,000 outlets with the power of a hundred plus salesmen, watch by watch, post which travel the entire route outlet by outlet all over again to ensure collections are in place. This is because most products are sold on credit.

But if it were a Rolex or Omega, they would have just *one store.* Two or three is pushing it.

Customers pay in *advance.*

Sometimes wait for years.

And spend a hundred or even a thousand times more than what they would for an equally good watch of a less celebrated brand. And as they walk away, heady with the notion that a favour has been bestowed upon them with an opportunity to conquer the world by simply being the possessor of the brand, we clearly understand they have not just bought a timepiece but way beyond that.

This is the story of how legends are created.

They stamp their presence and authority in a quietly confident manner. Whatever they ideate, even if it were mundane, they transform it into a work of art and an achievement that signifies something legendary and echoes with the whole world.

Hans Wilsdorf, the genius behind Rolex, knew that in creating a legend, he also transferred the legendary status to everyone who wore a Rolex.

This yearning is what makes people queue up at stores in the wee hours even in sub-zero temperatures to be the first to get their hands on an iPhone. Makes people dig into their savings to cough up ten times the price of a normal shoe just to have a Nike on their feet.

Even if someone were to create the most impressive features that match up to a Nike shoe, with all the accompanying benefits and at one-third the price, they would not be heard.

Because Nike is beyond those features.

Because Nike does not sell shoes.

The other day as I was closing my office, this young lad came running in with great excitement. He saw me leave and, almost breathlessly, said, "Sir, I have some amazing news. I have created an app with loads of newer and better features than Instagram and some freebies too. What do you think?" Not wanting to disappoint him, I appreciated his effort but told him I was in a hurry and would meet him a few days later. I knew that if this were his trajectory, he would be adding features by the dozen but still be struggling to generate the first hundred users, let alone be a challenge to the giant.

The most common mistake businesses make is believing they can create a legend or become the next phenomenon just by adding a plethora of features. Suppose features were the magic wand, in an industry such as watches where time is the sole and immutable function, an Omega can never price itself a thousand times more than a humbler counterpart which does the job equally well.

Quiz ten people on the street the reason for this considerable premium and they might well casually respond, "That's because Omega is a brand."

That is saying nothing.

That is akin to saying 'something sells because it sells'.

A brand, therefore, is the *effect* and *not the cause* of a product or service's unique offering and, thereby, its enormous success. Created by a special re-wiring of the mind.

Not recognising this precise cause-and-effect equation is the greatest fallacy of the hundreds of businesses and start-ups that fall by the wayside on the road to immortality. They create products with fantastic features, excellent benefits and impressive technology and still wonder why they have not been able to storm the market. It could be as outlandish as developing a technology that can transform the television into an oven, not realising that all they are doing is stepping on a treadmill they can never get off.

For every feature and technological innovation, there will be someone who can do it better. That is a given. It could be in a year, six months or even a day.
How often have you not heard an entrepreneur lament that the technology had become obsolete by the time they created the product!

Finally, the battle gets reduced to the 5-letter word...PRICE!

Did it ever make you wonder why only two companies in the entire world, yes, the entire world, can mix sugar and water and make you and me drink it?
And this has not been happening for a short five or ten summers but for an unbelievable 130-odd years! Considering that even the greatest innovations of science and technology have evolved and changed hands and are not the sole possession of any one person or company, this seems like a total revolution. While we all know it is not. So, what makes Coca-Cola, the $98 billion brand in 2022[1], rule for nearly two centuries and remain at the coveted No. 1 position whilst selling something that seems almost pedestrian?
As I mentioned earlier, in an era of the 'start-up bug' where a thousand companies sprout only to be swept aside by the first sign of a challenge, external or internal, a unique 'secretive' factor stands out.
A secret that makes a few ride the high wave for centuries, withstanding onslaughts of nature and business and selling simple products that anyone can manufacture but probably never sell even with all the advertising money in the world.

Colgate-Palmolive selling toothpaste for 150 years; Nestle selling coffee for over 150 years; Johnson & Johnson selling baby products for 135 years; Procter & Gamble selling Cold rub and sanitary pads for over one hundred years and Nike selling shoes for seventy years.

Simple products. Yet, dominating the market for scores of years.

Take a pause here.

Now is the moment of reflection for you. As you embark on a journey of entrepreneurship. To know that it is in this that lies the greatest difference.

It is not about which products you sell. It is not about how many more features your products possess than your competitor. It is not even about any great heritage or else two of the most reputed companies with enviable heritage in the telecom space would not have come spiralling down, despite selling the most advanced technology. Only because they had focussed on mere features and that volatile word, *price*.

It is about something else.

That 'something else' makes one stand out and shine almost forever. Even if they were to sell ordinary products. Even if a thousand pandemics came along the way to shake up their roots.

Before we embark on that 'something else', let us take a detour.

Around 4 p.m. on a cloudy day, a young girl places a panic call to the local TV service centre, urgently seeking help before 7 p.m. that same evening.

This sets the service person navigating a difficult terrain of fields and mountains with enormous effort and he finally spots the faint light coming from one of the small houses in a tiny hamlet.

Arriving at the door, he stands stupefied as a *blind girl* greets and guides him to the living room, where a silent TV awaits to be set right.

He spends the next few minutes in that hostel for the blind and gets the TV humming minutes before the 7 p.m. deadline. Then come streaming down all the other blind girls in excitement as they turn the TV on for their favourite channel. There, streaming from across thousands of miles, comes to life one of the hostel's favourite girls, a singer on a popular Indian music show.

Everyone joins the chorus. The moment is magical. As the SAMSUNG service specialist walks away in true joy and happiness at something more than just a job fulfilled, it is a moment that stops time and etches in you and me the true meaning and purpose of life.

Watch the commercial at: https://www.youtube.com/watch?v=779KwjAYTeQ&t=4s

SAMSUNG** conveys that **it is NOT merely in the business of television repair.

*So, **what business is it 'really' in?***

Shifting the focus to yet another landscape of the legends. An octogenarian who has just recovered from a stroke is seen in the bathroom with his sixty-year-old son performing a tender ritual. With the utmost delicate care, the son navigates a razor across his father's cheeks, shaving his stubble in the gentlest of manners ensuring the blade is almost like a feather smoothly caressing his skin. As the son explains the delight of this act, in making his father get the best treatment with this gesture, the sheer joy and ecstasy of this beautiful father-son relationship captivate one and all.

It is a commercial for GILLETTE.

Watch: https://www.youtube.com/watch?v=Rkik9ffBN1o&t=3s.

The commercial had no mention of how the razor possessed better features than any other brand. Not a single reference to how excellent the product was. Not even a statement of how that particular shaving instrument had an enviable track record.

Why?

Because ***GILLETTE is NOT in the business of shaving instruments.***

What business is it 'really' in?

Let us tune into a Christmas story.

A Christmas when a father had to travel to a faraway land leaving his young daughter in tears, to a lonely and empty festival. As his car is about to leave, the daughter runs across and hands him an envelope to be posted to Santa. The address: The North Pole. As he reaches his maritime workstation, he spots the sea post heading towards various destinations. Eager to get to them with the letter, he misses, falls into the sea, navigates the most torturous of terrains over the next few days and finally reaches Santa's house – only to find it locked. He dejectedly drops the letter there and takes a few steps to return. To his surprise, he sees a Coca-Cola truck waiting to take him back to his workplace. Many hours later, to his utter amazement, he finds the vehicle dropping him off at his own house.

Perplexed by the turn of events, he stands transfixed as the driver hands him the letter his daughter had earlier given him. He opens it to read. Written inside is his daughter's wish: "*Please bring home my daddy for Christmas.*"

Turning around, he sees his daughter running into his arms.

That was a ***COCA-COLA*** commercial.

Watch:https://www.youtube.com/watch?v=yg4Mq5EAEzw&t=2s

Nothing about how tasty the drink was. Nothing about how it can quench the thirst of millions in a unique manner. Nothing about how it is different from all other drinks.

Just this story.

Clearly, ***COCA-COLA is NOT in the business of soft drinks. So, what business is it 'really' in?***

Have you ever wondered what makes you walk in repeatedly into ***STARBUCKS*** and pay astronomical sums for a cup of coffee which may not be the world's best? Which could pale in comparison to the taste and flavour of a Rs.30 Madras café coffee in your neighbourhood?

Because ***STARBUCKS,*** while it makes coffee and sells coffee, ***is NOT in the business of coffee.*** Surprised?

One of the reasons you often find that you may not be disturbed for hours even without placing an order unless you make it a habit of using that space for free!

What business is, therefore, Starbucks 'really' in?

Did it ever occur to you that ***Royal Enfield (BULLET) is NOT in the business of motorcycles?***

No? If it were really in the business of motorcycles, it would have been wiped out in a few years as many others would have claimed a better space in the customer's mind with price and almost similar, if not far more advanced features.

So, what business is Royal Enfield 'really' in?

And here lies the secret sauce:

SAMSUNG is NOT in the business of television repair.
It is in the business of compassion, empathy and care.

GILLETTE is NOT in the business of razors.
It represents a man who goes beyond the realm of what all other men do and shows his profound love and care, with the strongest of familial bonds and values.
It is in the business of love and commitment to a cause.

COCA-COLA is NOT in the business of soft drinks.
It is in the business of togetherness and love.

STARBUCKS is in the ***business of providing a welcoming, uninterruptible meeting space for executives to make decisions.***

That is its 'real' business.

Royal Enfield is in the ***business of providing a spirit of freedom, a spirit of adventure, self-expression, self-worth, passion, independence, pride and power.***

While ***JOHNSON & JOHNSON*** has extremely expensive products dedicated to babies, it is not in the business of these baby products.

It is in the business of enhancing and representing an extension of a mother's love for her child.

Moments of love. Moments that are priceless. Moments that make life worth dying for.

These are the 'real' businesses they all are in.

All these brands have one commonality. Can you recognise that commonality?

The commonality of never dwelling on features. Nor on any benefits.

Pause here and reflect on what this commonality is that makes them the giants they are. That has made them leaders in their field for years on end. Casting away the ravages of nature, environment, people and situations for eternity, maybe facing a pandemic or two on the way, but never deterred. And are forever at that enviable No.1 Position. And sometimes selling just ordinary products which anyone could manufacture.

So, what is it that they do so differently from ordinary mortals?

Stop! Reflect and fill in your answer here. Now!

If you cracked it, you are on the fast track to success.
The legends are the giants for this sole reason.
They understand and immaculately create a *TIMELESS* factor, one which is competition- and adversity-proof. That makes them UNSTOPPABLE.

That factor, in a word, is EMOTION.

The Timeless Factor that the legends have understood and constantly work everything around is

EMOTION

Hence when they embark on the science of the unconquerable by asking an all-important but never really asked question, 'What business are we really in?' the answer stands out prominently.
Because the question they actually address is, *"What emotional business are we really in?"*
Because the legends have understood that emotion is the only timeless and changeless reality that not just defines us as human beings but scripts our DNA.
A Stanford Professor's research showed that not 70 per cent, not 80 per cent but almost 95 per cent of every action we take is based on emotion and we justify it later using the rationale route.[2] That, you would agree, is not a percentage to be taken lightly.

"Every decision is made long before our awareness can fabricate a retrospective reason for it."-Tim Ash

And the decision is always made based on EMOTION.

Why is emotion timeless?

With time, most things in the world have changed. How we cut across oceans or the blue skies in just a few hours is extraordinary. That we can virtually be present with someone a thousand miles away is a thought that would have been unimaginable even a few decades ago.

And here is a peek at a few other startling changes with time.

The MODALITY of communication, from handwritten, paper-based letters, surrendered into the hands of the dutiful postman to being delivered in the form of a few emojis on the mobile device, has changed.

This is obvious.

But some changes are far more subtle yet powerfully different.

I still remember my mother writing long letters and waiting nearly 21 days for a reply. It would take seven days for the letter to reach me from Chennai and another seven days for her to receive a reply from me at IIT Kanpur, Occasionally, I would not respond right away and this lapse in filial duty, however unintentional, further added to the delay.

Fast forward to now. We send a message at 8.32 a.m. and at 8.44 a.m., if we fail to receive a response, especially if the 'last seen' was 8.38 a.m., our mind goes into a frenzy. "Does she still love me?" "Did I say something wrong to my boss?" Cortisol (the stress chemical) is in full flow here!

The expectation of the speed of response has changed.

Those were the days when we travelled to faraway lands and returned after weeks without the exchange of a single word of communication. Maybe a single, hurried phone call. No going into overdrive about whether we were taken hostage by an alien who came in from the dark or whisked away to an unknown destination by a foreign enchantress. There was complete confidence and faith that all was well.

Once again, fast forward to 2023.

Look at the bizarre flow of messages when someone takes on a short trip.

Leave home: 8.15 a.m.

"Got into the cab": 8.25 a.m.

"On the way": 8.45 a.m.

"Reached airport": 9.30 a.m.

"Checked in": 9.45 a.m.

"Waiting to board": 10.15 a.m.

"Boarded": 10.30 a.m.

"Taking off": 10.45 a.m.

"Landed": 12 noon.

And an equal few from the corresponding part of the world till one reaches the hotel. A barrage of close to eighteen messages by the time one reaches the destination.

Phew! What has changed?

The intensity of communication has changed.

The faith in ourselves and the universe has changed. And certainly not for the better!

However, a few things have not changed.

When with bated breath, you hold the mobile device and pray intensely for that long-awaited call from a dear one and when

it finally rings, you feel a rush inside you that makes you miss a heartbeat.
That feeling hasn't changed. ***LOVE***

You are walking down a lonely road one night and there is a slight hint of rain. You suddenly hear footsteps behind and soon they become faster and nearer. You try to muster up all the courage not to look back and continue. But still, your mind races towards all those Netflix stories of a night stalker. A strange feeling is gripping your chest.
That feeling hasn't changed. ***FEAR***

You are driving to work on a busy Monday morning and are increasingly becoming late for that all-important meeting. As you weave through the never-ending traffic, that sleek BMW sports car cuts in and takes off, almost making you miss an accident.
At that moment, you could have killed the driver if you could have gotten hold of him.
That feeling hasn't changed. ***ANGER***

Bangalore airport. 7 p.m. Boarding has just been announced. And it is time. For you to let go of her hand and say goodbye. Not knowing when you will see her again. As she walks towards the gate, words seem to choke in your throat. It is going to be a long drive back home. Alone.
That feeling hasn't changed. ***SADNESS***

Over the years, while a myriad things around us have changed significantly, what has been ***timeless*** *is* what was and will always be ***within us.***

The one that makes us dream. The one that makes us dare. The one that makes life worth living. And sometimes worth giving up. And the one that makes us rise to levels of becoming ***Unstoppable.***

That is EMOTION.

So, whenever you create an entity using FAB (Features, Attributes and Benefits), you create a PRODUCT.
A product whose features can be bettered by someone at a later point, as I mentioned earlier.
You will then inadvertently be transferring the 'power' to the customer.
The customer will then constantly challenge and haunt you and present you with ten other 'products' with better features and lower prices. You will then forever be in defensive mode, eventually losing the race in the never-ending pit of 'price' from where you can never rise.

The legends recognise this flaw and hence play their game on something eternal.
Something ***changeless.*** *That gives them that edge to remain forever ahead.*

And that is EMOTION.

Emotion is that frequency that transfers the burden of defending the product to the customer and voila, it sets you free!

THIS IS THE BIGGEST SECRET OF ALL THE LEGENDS.
Known only to a few. And now, putting you among those few.

The Reversibility Effect

Here is the biggest bonus. Something truly interesting happens when you weave an emotion around what you offer the customer. When the customer feels *that specific emotion* in an entirely different situation, one of the cells in the brain will light up to subtly summon up your product or service. This is known as the *'Reversibility Effect'*.

Let me explain. For example, if the emotion of 'pride' is stoked in you when you come across a particular brand and later, the emotion of 'pride' surfaces in you in an entirely unrelated situation – the brain will still *connect the emotion of pride in this situation with the brand* you had seen some time earlier. In the quietest of manners, that product or service will come to the fore at the subconscious level.

In essence

PRODUCTS DO NOT SELL.

ONLY EMOTIONS DO.

When someone claims to have created a 'brand' they effectively refer to converting a product into an *emotion*, thereby making that space in the mind where one associates that product not so much with its functional value but something beyond. They have virtually carved out a place where a 'price' cannot be tagged, thus, making it impregnable and incomparable. Hence, customers will now defend the brand as they begin to take ownership.

This emotional integration is the process of how a BRAND is created.

And this is how legends have established themselves in history. Not by advertising. Not by flanking the product with celebrities. Not by offering a hundred features more than competitors. But through the metamorphosis of that product essence into a changeless emotion.

This insight is the foundation of a business's transformation into a legendary one.

Asking this all-important question:

'What emotional business am I really in?'

You are never in the business of tiles, software, automobiles, furniture, mobile phones, TVs, pharmaceuticals or any specific product group. If you are, your journey is only ephemeral and will need constant sustenance and push, thus tying you with a leash to your business, which you will never be able to shake off.

They will always be *products* that will only help you reach a particular place.

Those businesses which make you go beyond the realm of the ordinary and cross over into the exclusive world of iconic brands that define and differentiate you will revolve around that all-important question of ***"What emotional business are you 'really' in?"***

No amount of finance, HR or manufacturing advancements and intelligence can help if you get this insight wrong.

The biggest secret in the journey from the land of the ordinary to that of the greatest brands and legends is the transition from ***a product business to an emotional business.***

This discernment is the key to eternity.

Having established this premise about the true business that you need to be in, another question will pop up.

"Amidst the myriad emotions, how does one decide which emotion one needs to invoke in the customer?"

In our company, IntouchConsulting.In, we undertook extensive research on this subject with over two hundred people in different geographical and demographic cultures to unearth this answer.

What we found was quite revealing.

Of the thousands of emotions that affect us, there are essentially *only two emotions that drive us.*

LOVE

FEAR

Love is the emotion that propels one forward and fear is the one that holds us back.

Every emotion you see would fall into one of these two categories.

This recognition, while revealing, could be complicated for someone looking at that distinct and precise emotion associated exclusively with one's offering.

A further deep dive provides the answer that is the need of the hour.

Keeping fear aside, a negative emotion I do not advocate, the following emotions ranked high as the most stirring ones within the sphere of LOVE.

Various external stimuli lead to the underlying emotions of love and desire. The emotions that have therefore stood out as the ones covering over ninety per cent of our innermost drives are:

1. **Pride**

A tremendous sense of fulfilment of having attained something exceptional, either material or otherwise. A sense that sends the signal of loving oneself and is the antithesis of fear.

2. **Recognition**

People always seek external stimuli to ratify who they are. To reaffirm their sense of their true identity. To ensure they are 'being loved.'

3. **Aspiration**

To 'rise' to a level far higher than one's current status in any field has always been a significant factor in the hierarchy of human needs. It is a desire that springs from the core of love for the self within.

4. **Inspiration**

This is yet again a place where one 'strives' to be a better version of oneself with the sole objective of deriving a sense of deep, personal love.

5. **Self-Worth**

Needless to say, this forms the core of one's being and that is rooted in nothing other than love. Even emotions such as sexual desire stem from this feeling, while in a larger context, this 'self' can have connotations of an overall sense of oneness.

6. **Trust**

Can anything be more important in life than trust? Trust in oneself and others comes from the deep bond born out of almost unconditional love.

Trust, in many cases, impels the person to perform actions beyond the rational realm with the most profound faith, which can only result from love.

7. **Nostalgia**

Nostalgia is proof of love both for oneself and for an earlier personal moment, reminiscing about which generates joy and love. The need to feel the past in your present with the most profound happiness. Ironically, when that 'past' was the 'present', it may or may not have been such a source of joy.

8. **Freedom**

This is yet another powerful driver which generates in us all the relevant emotions of independence, joy and ecstasy that stem from the core emotion of 'love'. A sense of not being 'tied' to anything, a person, situation or even a thought, is a liberating feeling. Hence *freedom*, while it may not be traditionally classified as an emotion, has a decisive role to play.

Attaining these or being deprived of them leads to the manifestation of sub-emotions such as joy, sadness, anger, excitement and a few others.

The fascinating news is that all these emotions are business-agnostic in that they have the same impact on a completely new product, an existing one, a B2B, B2C, a B2B2C or even D2C (Direct to customer) type of business.

These emotions can also be integrated into *any offering.* It could be consumer non-durables, durables, pharmaceuticals, services of any kind, telecom and *every avenue* the mind can conceive of. These emotions are also *valid across continents,* whether one is in India, USA, Africa or the Middle East and *across demographics,* whether one is a baby boomer, a millennial or a Gen Z.

Transcending the Unique Power of Three

I had mentioned in the earlier chapter that in any category if three brands currently dominate a particular product space, it is near impossible to penetrate that market. And if those three brands have captured the space *with specific individual emotions,* it would be a Herculean task for a new entrant to make a mark in that segment, even with better features or benefits.

This is irrespective of how the three brands fall short on features or benefits and maybe not even adhere to their original brand promise. But if the following strategy is adopted, the new entrant can circumvent the above limitation.

Since specific emotions are already associated with the space, you need to *create a new emotion that strongly overrides the current emotions* in that space. Or if the current brands are failing in their emotional offering, offer that emotion in a strong and visible manner.

In the example of the app-based taxi-hailing system mentioned earlier, the critical emotional offering was *convenience,* translating into the emotion of peace of mind through less stress.

In reality, some of the current brands in the app-based taxi service space have clearly missed catering to that emotion of convenience. They now border on creating an emotion of insecurity, uncertainty and stress where the customer is in the dark regarding the cab they have booked –will it actually turn up or send a 'cancelled' message?

In this case of a brand failing on the emotional offering, as evidenced by the taxi-hailing app space, *a newer entry now has the unique opportunity to gain a foothold in that same emotional space*. The possibilities are many, as we see new entrants such as MY^{n} recognising this gap. Only time will tell of their ability to grasp this hidden truth and their determination to translate it into actionable deliverables.

The cardinal principle before entering a category, if you are an entrepreneur, is to ensure you never enter a segment where it is already represented by 'three great brands.'

But if you still choose to enter such a category, you should be better prepared to perform the following two tests.

1. Are the three well-established companies representing powerful emotional businesses? And is the audience large enough for those emotions? Suppose the answer is negative in either of the two conditions, which is extremely unlikely, you should explore through research what emotions will have a telling effect on the various audience segments that could make them swerve towards a newer brand option.

2. If the category is already represented by emotional businesses strongly, which is more likely the case, conduct

in-depth research on consumer preferences. It may reveal an opportunity regarding an emotion that is missing or not being fulfilled in this space (for example, in our earlier taxi-hailing app system, 'trust' could be a missing emotion). You can then utilise that knowledge to leverage that emotion to your advantage. Of course, this journey would be fraught with enormous challenges since it would not be a comfortable ride to dethrone someone firmly entrenched. But that's the journey legends will not be afraid to take.

Which Horse to Ride?

As you embark on the entrepreneurial journey, you will come to a bend where you will be faced with a unique question: 'Which horse should I mount and ride?'

One option is to ride horses with the most muscular legs, thus striding across paths and horizons with absolute ease, which is the narrative I have described of the famed brands up to now. Brands whose tenacity and grit to go up the 'Golden Ladder' is far greater than any downward pull of any pandemic.

Or you could ride another type of horse too.

While this certainly is outside the scope of this book, it may be pertinent to mention yet another horse based on an emerging model, fuelled by greed and short-term results. While a few do have merit in value creation, the majority in this model ride the horse of valuations based on flimsy and unwanted routes cloaked in sensationalism, sometimes with false promises, as a hack to generate Venture Capital (VC) funding. These brands then use those dollars for awareness and user base generation, only to exit at the first available opportunity with the objective of the 'Get Rich Quick Schemes' (GRQS).

Examples of such businesses range from those shouting themselves hoarse about bringing a relatively unimportant service to your doorstep in just seven minutes, only to use the excuse of traffic when they do not honour the promise. But having created enough sensationalism to gain traction and thereby funding, they could use the funds to fuel an entirely different promise of offering products at a discount, which was never the original problem they claimed to solve.

Not surprisingly, all it requires to bring that 'seven-minute delivery' model down and eclipse its presence is a new campaign by a competitor with the claim of delivering in six minutes!

When celebrations are being planned for a big wedding, you will not be the most popular person if you were to ask the couple what their divorce strategy is. That is the same, in my opinion, as planning an exit strategy even before you start a new venture, which most of these companies indulge in.

This again goes back to the core 'why' you are taking this on. The above strategy could be for those individuals whose prime goal is to make a few quick bucks and move on. But that will not be the direction or purpose for individuals wanting to leave a lasting legacy. The legends that this book is aimed at creating.

I have mentioned this only to highlight the GRQ start-up ecosystem that is probably emerging and most certainly outside the purview of this book.

The Need to Match Emotion with the Audience

Now that we have discussed the first and all-important milestone of recognising the *criticality of transforming any business into an emotional one*, yet another vital factor needs to be addressed. This factor is the singular focus through which to create, among the select emotions described, *that specific emotion which resonates most with the largest segment of the target audience*. If this is not done accurately, all efforts will pale.

Remember the recent movie *83?*

A film that was launched to replicate the memories of 1983 when India, against all incredible odds, pulled off the World Cup victory for the very first time in cricket?

The hype for the movie was huge, the stories the media created were larger than life and the expectation was for one of the greatest box office successes, with all the best stars roped in. It was an excellent product with all the perfect ingredients for stupendous success. But as the movie was released, I went on to express my thoughts on social media on how this could never be one of the all-time greats. Despite the wrath of many a supporter of that movie, eventually, I was proved right.

Why was I right?

Because on an extremely crucial parameter, the movie was way off target.

At half past twelve, one midnight in that eventful year, as Mohinder Amarnath ran in to bowl to Michael Holding of West Indies, struggling at 146 for nine, thirty-seven runs behind India's score of 183, most Indians were waiting with bated breath. As Holding was declared LBW, the whole country fell silent for a moment in utter disbelief, only to erupt in a joy that echoed through the night across every city of India. India, who had not even been expected to go beyond the first two matches, had won the World Cup! For the first time in the history of the game! Thus in 1983, when India managed to pull off that miracle, the *emotion* overflowing all over the country was *PRIDE*, the first of which I had mentioned as the *eight key emotions* earlier.

But by 2022, India had done that and more. Pride had already been tasted. It was not an emotion that could lend itself to the same cause. Hence the emotion of pride was not attempted to be replicated. So, in my opinion, the producers shifted the emphasis to the other all-important emotion of *NOSTALGIA*. This 'emotion realignment' was their error in judgement as only that section of the audience who were supporters way back in 1983 could feel the nostalgia. That restricted the audience mainly to the sixty-plus age bracket. That was only about thirty per cent of it. The remaining seventy per cent, under the age of thirty-five, unfortunately, could not feel nostalgia for the victory as it was way before they were born.

Suddenly the audience the movie was addressing was not even a tenth of the Indian population. With the 'die-hard' fans of cricket being an even smaller fraction, the total addressable market was extremely low. Additionally, even the mega stars of the movie could not pull in the masses, despite their large fan following in the younger age bracket. Because these masses, whom the stars were wowing, had little affiliation with an event that occurred much before their time, for them to make the effort to reach the theatres.

While the movie did not do badly, it fell short of all the huge expectations at the box office.

All because:

The emotion was not synchronised with the size of the audience. The chosen emotion was aimed at an insufficient portion of the target audience both in size and context.

So, the foundational principle is that beyond scripting the exact emotion, it must be coordinated with the relevant audience to achieve that magical effect.

Here is a contra example.

In the world of JUICES, dominated by titans such as Tropicana, Real and Maaza, where it was almost impossible to penetrate, arrived an upstart (aka start-up) which not only entered with gumption but also reached the top very soon.

PAPER BOAT

Paper Boat never focussed solely on features such as 'fibre'. Paper Boat never laid emphasis on the benefit of 'taste.' The last priority in Paper Boat's terminology was 'price.'

All Paper Boat communicated, in a first-person narrative, was, "When I was young, I picked up this paper, folded it into a boat, walked to the riverside, placed it on the water and watched it float."

No features. No benefits. Only sheer emotion. And the emotion: **NOSTALGIA.**

Paper Boat clearly got the calculation perfectly correct. The people who identified with this nostalgic memory encompassed *most age groups* since, in this case, the emotion of nostalgia touched almost everyone.

The emotion of nostalgia in this example, unlike the movie *83*, was not directed towards a specific event which would have demographic limitations but one that tugged at the hearts of everyone.

Amazing insight!

The above two studies clearly demonstrate how the same emotion, when managed differently based on meshing or otherwise with the relevant audience, produces contrary yet dramatic results.

One statement that is constantly posed to me is, "This power of emotion to create something incredible is valid in B2C. Not sure if it can stand its ground in the B2B segment."

Nothing could be farther from the truth. A survey conducted by Google CEB said that seven-ninths of B2B companies engage emotionally with their customers over 50 per cent of the time.[3]
Research from Les Binet and Peter Field for the B2B segment claim that B2B strategies that appeal to emotion are seven times more effective[4].
Fifty-nine per cent of European sellers say that emotion is one of the top factors in their business and a specific one.

The common fallacy: Regarding B2B, most question the possibility of an emotional transaction if a company ABC sells its services to another company XYZ. The flaw lies in the fact that *company* ABC would not sell to *company* XYZ. Instead, an *individual human* at ABC would work to ink the deal with another *individual human* at XYZ.

You sell to people. To humans. Never to corporations and organisations. *Humans sell to humans*. Both at the delivering and the receiving end are humans with definite and palpable emotions. With a clearly earmarked psychological profile for that *role and designation*. Every decision emanates from a place where the primary driver is emotion.

Every time an organisation has bought into something, there is a human at the other end with various personal and professional aspirations that come into play. This complexity makes B2B challenging but probably the most satisfying.

Look at **VOLVO**, the company that manufactures trucks. It cannot get more B2B than this. Large, unwieldy and extremely expensive machines sold to transport companies and other institutions.

In the most *defying* manner, Volvo embarked on a live test showing Van Damme, actor and martial artist, performing an epic leg split that made everyone watch with absolute amazement. In the live demonstration dramatised even more astonishingly, he stood with his legs apart, one leg each on two different moving Volvo trucks. Requiring precision beyond the wildest dreams, the demonstration reflected the combined emotions of the artiste's *courage and trust* in the vehicle's capability.

Volvo worked on the emotions of the customer on two fronts simultaneously. One is *trust.* Nothing could convey confidence in the product more powerfully than what was demonstrated visually – trust in precision of the highest nature.

The second is *inspiration.* It also inspired every individual to emulate *the person* seen performing such a heart-stopping stunt.

Thus, satisfying both the personal and professional needs of that 'individual human', making the buying decision, with *emotional* ease.

It is almost impossible to imagine a more complex and intricate entity on the B2B canvas than **CATERPILLAR**. A company in the business of heavy 'earth-moving' equipment. Many would scorn the notion that emotion could be the core of their business.

The brand *defied* that notion.

Through stunning communication, it created a narrative wherein it integrated the emotion of *nostalgia and trust* by producing a commercial in which its large excavator machines simulated the children's game of Jenga, executing all the moves with astonishing precision and skill.

Every element in that film conveyed the emotions of trust and nostalgia to the buyer's mind. *Trust* at the professional level and *nostalgia* on the individual's front. Of course, achieving this emotional integration in such a heavy B2B product segment requires exceptional creativity and thorough understanding of the audience. *But that is what makes legends stand out from the ordinary.*

One can never forget how a minor component in a giant device transformed the way it was perceived and led to the product's dependency on it, when it was actually intended to be the other way.

INTEL did not want to be just one of the components inside the giant hearts of a PC. And this was not easy. But it chose *to dare*: Find the impossible. Convert the business of chip manufacturing into an emotional one of trust. This made it unique. Or else it would have been fighting over price and scrabbling for survival, if it managed to exist at all.

But today, it stands tall, almost unassailable, in its field. And is UNSTOPPABLE.

What, then, would be the driving factors in the emotional business of B2B?

From all the examples above, three areas stand out.

The *first,* the driving emotion, is undoubtedly *trust.* With billing values being extraordinarily high and spread over longer terms, *trust* outweighs all others as the number one factor. When that trust is established, scaling the many mountains in the relationship becomes easier and ensures its longevity.

I recently returned to the store where I had purchased a piece of jewellery for my daughter because it developed a patina it should not have. While the store owner was all honey and sugar,

she tried to write off the worrying black marks as a reaction to the box it was packaged in rather than admitting it was due to an incorrect setting on their part. This approach erodes trust because of the *second* and far-reaching factor, *transparency.*
Many fear transparency for the harm it may do them. Unfortunately, the converse is true. Transparency enhances trust. *And lack of transparency kills it.*

HOOTSUITE, a company integrating multiple social media platforms on a single dashboard, suddenly found itself embroiled in a spate of criticism. Rather than brushing it under the carpet, it overcame the crisis most innovatively and effectively – through a campaign of self-deprecation. Each of its employees read out tweets from consumers deriding the user interface (UI) of the product, adding an element of humour to the barrage of criticism. By highlighting the very aspect, it was blamed for, not only did Hootsuite underline that it was a truly transparent business, but it also enhanced the relationship by conveying it was 'listening' to the customer.
Trust and transparency lead to the *third* and final feather in the cap of business success: *Credibility.*
There can be severe implications for a B2B business, even if an iota of credibility comes under suspicion.

It is not surprising that a B2B customer is willing to pay up to eight times the premium if they can see personal value enhancement. However, they may never return if any emotional ingredients are open to doubt.

SAGE, one of the six companies which was slated to be the best brand of 2022 (*Marketing Week*), is a full-scale software organisation. The words of their CMO, Cath Keers, clearly indicate that the decisions on software and payroll are "very emotional" and she agrees with the opinion that there is nothing such as B2B. It is a *human selling to a human all the time.*

When you recognise that there is a human with personal emotions and ambitions at the other end and you address those simultaneously, you genuinely have touched the soul of B2B. That person in that specific position who wants to make a difference to themselves *and* to the organisation will be driven by individual concerns and aspirations derived primarily from *emotion,* apart from the domain requirements of the business.

TSI Power, a company in Vadodara, India, whom I was advising, has made a mark for itself in the B2B business of high-precision automatic voltage regulators. TSI prided itself on its product detecting an anomaly in power transmission in *twenty milliseconds*, thereby saving millions of dollars for the customer.

It was a brilliant technological innovation – with one risk. While the proposition was true, the company was unknowingly heading down the path of the feature-based strategy where a rival claiming they could do the same job in *fifteen* milliseconds could put it out of business.

By recognising that B2B is actually a P2P -person-to-person -too and that there were personal and professional needs of the person at the other end, we put together the actual emotional business they were in.

One of the biggest problems TSI's potential clients faced, apart from the long-term longevity reduction of the high-end machines, was their sudden failure and the need for the supervisor-in-charge to be on standby, even at night. Every night. That was not something anyone would desire. These machine failures not only disrupted the supervisor's peace but were also a constant concern leading to unwanted stress.

By eradicating this, TSI could provide sleep and peace of mind to the supervisor.

Thus, its business transited from just providing a tech solution (which could be transcended any time) to the *emotional business of providing **peace of mind*** through its incredibly high-quality products. Companies shy away from the effort of converting a B2B business into an emotional one, purely because of their limited understanding of who the actual customer is, requiring a greater sense of creativity than B2C.

But the ones who dive into this are the ones who will find that magical pearl.

Do This ACTION Exercise Now!

It is that time when you need to pause and reflect deeply on what business, at an emotional level, you really are in.

Put it down in as much detail as possible.

Check if that emotion is an integral part of the audience you are catering to. Ensure the audience size is in sync with your vision expectations.

MANTRA 5

WHOSE NAME IS IT ANYWAY?

The Brand Christening

WHAT'S IN A NAME?

"

Names are but the outward expression of the soul of things.

In a small hamlet on the outskirts of Bangalore, in the wee hours, a child's cry splits the silence of the night. Suddenly there is a tremendous amount of excitement. Many lights are turned on. Whispers turn into mumblings and finally into loud bursts of joy.

Yes, a baby is born. She had arrived to the music of ecstasy. Over the next few weeks, there is joyous activity as everyone in the family is solely occupied with the baby's naming ceremony. A few recommend religious lineages while a few others advocate carrying on the elders' bloodline and the rest are busy glorifying adjectives of nature and strengths of various kinds.

Finally, the auspicious day arrives. The child is laid in the cradle or in the mother's lap. At a function surpassed in grandeur only by an Indian wedding, the name is whispered in the baby's ear and inscribed on a bed of rice. Conches are blown and blessings are showered on the baby with turmeric-smeared grains of rice as prayers and invocation of Grace from the Gods mark this moment of greatness.

A name had been created and etched in history.

On the other hand, in the offices of the high street, when one embarks on this ambitious thought of creating value for an audience through a product, why should its christening be any less in splendour and grandeur when this corporate 'baby' is born? Like that of an infant's naming ceremony.
This name, in future, could be the synonym of success, similar to Apple, Nike, Coke, Tanishq or Amul.

So, a name defines you. It characterises everything about you. It is what creates all the mental imagery when it is uttered, in all its psychological and other connotations.

Replace the name Apple or Nike with another and the organisation will likely go defunct soon.
Such is the power that a name finally acquires.
Thus, a name is the beginning of everything; in many cases, it *continues* to be everything.
It is highly doubtful that you would elicit the response "it does not matter" when you ask anyone their name. It is always the most prized possession of any human being and the sweetest

music to one's ears. Do you realise that just the recollection of someone's name evokes all the various feelings and emotions associated with that person?

Unfortunately, many do not take this all-important name factor seriously enough, only to regret it later.

This MANTRA is the journey into the science of what makes name creation unique and timeless.

So, how does one decide on a name?

When one observes the names of some of the most successful Indian brands, Tanishq, Aquaguard, Airtel, Reliance and Amul or global legends such as Nike, Jaguar and Montblanc, there is a clear pattern that emerges.

While this could be different in the case of service brands such as Dunzo, OYO or Zomato, a commonality is constantly visible across the others.

Let us explore that a bit more.

The main difference between product and service names is the frequency of usage, with the latter scoring higher. However, fast moving consumer goods (FMCG) which are used with far higher frequency compete as strongly on that count.

As I had mentioned and affirmed earlier, the key to success lies only in one element.

The ability to convert your product or service business into an emotional business. And that journey begins here.

Starting here is the best form to achieve that objective. Emotion is not something that is triggered only in a single avenue. The more consistent its application, the greater its integration into the consumer's mind. Thus, when one hears the name, *if it can trigger the same emotion the business is attempting to portray*, what better start could there be?

A couple of weeks ago, I had a friend come over who wanted to chat about a start-up product with which he was involved. He had been following my blogs, posts and videos on emotion's importance in converting a product into a legend.

So, when I asked him the product's name, he said excitedly, "I followed your advice on how it has to be emotionally integrated and hence I am calling it *Munpa*."

I was unsure I had heard him right, so I asked him to repeat it, only to hear him echo the same name. I asked him what it meant. He said, "The first three letters are from my name and the next two are from my wife's name, which has a great emotional connotation for us."

I could not believe what I heard and realised that he had missed a critical and essential component in the naming process.

I gently explained that the emotional connect must be directed towards what resonates with the customer and not the product's owner.

A trigger, in this case the name, must link the emotional business with the CUSTOMER's mind. Not with the founder. Or any of their partners.

TANISHQ

A jewellery brand that beat the odds to shine among the greats had this clearly narrated in its script. Tanishq is in the business of providing not just jewellery but *the emotional business* of 'enhancing the overall beauty and glamour of a woman through body and mind.'

In Hindi, the word '*tan*' refers to the body and 'ishq' connotes love. Another version has it that 'Nishk' refers to a gold ornament.

In either manner, Tanishq combines these two easily comprehensible words reflecting an emotional value while quickly creating a distinctive name.

What a start! What a story as it went on to vanquish everyone in its field!

NIKE

The name of the winged Greek goddess of Victory. Greeks are known for being great warriors. And when coupled with the Goddess of Victory, the emotion the name evokes is matchless. The Swoosh logo adds to the name with its connotations of speed, power and motivation.

AMUL

A derivative of 'Amulya', one that connotes the value and emotion of being ***precious or priceless***. In the business of milk and other dairy products, if what we ingest stems from the attribute of incomparable purity, making it 'precious', it is the perfect recipe for the crowning glory of a name.

APPLE

A unique and revolutionary representation. While there are many theories afloat regarding the origin, including one which connotes 'creation' given its provenance in the proverbial forbidden fruit, I strongly believe this has been the outcome of two robust thought processes. One, the name being 'outside of the ordinary' for electronic products and PCs triggers a tremendous, curiosity-based, 'word of mouth' communication. This strategy is an excellent start for a brand. Since Apple had surpassed every industry and brand standard in its sensational product and design offering at inception itself and required only recall, this curiosity element cemented its uniqueness.

The other reason is that 'apple' has often represented the highest or positive quality in several contexts. 'An apple a day keeps the doctor away' or 'she is the apple of everyone's eye' are just a few of the allusions from time immemorial that directly trigger your senses and kickstart the prefrontal cortex in your brain (the part responsible for emotion). The word 'apple' then brings to the fore all the pleasurable memories, activating the link to release dopamine, the pleasure chemical, thus transporting you to the land of the extraordinary.

So, when you embark on the name creation process, ask whether the following three factors would be fully taken care of for the name to get impregnated in the brain.

1. Functionality

If you can achieve the functionality factor in the name itself, you do not have to spend time, effort and dollars explaining what the product is. Many brands seem completely unaware of this and spend most of their time and finances 'explaining' their brand name, while only a select few are aware of the secret path to the customer's mind.

2. Emotionality

Once functionality has been taken care of, emotionality needs to be the driving force. I cannot overemphasise how critical this is; it has been the backbone of all we have discussed thus far and that sets the legends apart.

Emotionality ingrained in every element, starting with the name, earmarks the direction in the journey towards the unassailable.

3. Memorability

While this is an obvious no-brainer, ensuring your brand has an exceptionally high recall is important. You would obviously not find it easy to stir your memory bank with a name like 'Menorexa', for instance. There is just one among the trillion cells in our brains which needs to set aside this unsolicited information to bring it to the fore at the right time. Hence, every element needs to enhance that.

But it is not rare to see this being the main driver in multiple cases. Yes, memorability does play a crucial role in getting the brain cells ticking but concentrating on this alone poses dangers of a different kind. It may be worthwhile to share the following experience.

As I was driving through the crowded streets of Bangalore, my eyes went briefly to a large hoarding hollering out a brand's arrival. As I moved on, it was impossible to relate that name to either toothpaste, condom or travel service. The company thus had lost an excellent opportunity to effectively communicate what the name stood for, probably due to the over-emphasis on brevity and, thereby, the memorability of its name. While every business is screaming its presence from the rooftops for that all-important yet unavailable consumer attention, spending incredible amounts of money and not achieving the fundamental purpose seems like a terrible waste.

A few days later, another highway sign had me looking at the message under the same brand name I had seen earlier, announcing it was a 'camera brand.' Thus, the company required a minimum of two interactions before it even communicated what it was. If the brand managers felt it would make my heart skip a beat and have me dash to their nearest store, the ruse failed miserably.

A couple of days later, my attention was drawn to a larger-than-life-size poster of a famous actor. Adjacent to his picture was the image of the same product again! This entire exercise seemed so meaningless as all this did was create an awareness that, yet another variant of an existing category had joined the already crowded market shelves.

There is nothing incorrect with this method if financial considerations are neither relevant nor essential while generating consumer attention. But if they are, as they should be, both the factors of functionality and emotionality too could have been achieved if the name was woven around them. In the above example, all that was achieved was the customer's attention being repeatedly drawn to it to just create *awareness*. Scripting an emotional relationship was not even a consideration here.

Some recent examples that have taken the space of social media very effectively, such as LinkedIn and Facebook, have successfully understood the importance of the above-explained trio of functionality, emotionality and memorability in crafting their names.

Do This ACTION Exercise Now!
Take a few minutes to detail each of the three pillars of name creation: functionality, emotionality and memorability in these two social media platforms, LinkedIn and Facebook

A few start-ups aiming at the service-based app space take on the memorability factor alone. This can cover the distance if the start-up, as I had mentioned earlier, is riding the horse that mainly aims to create valuation through user traction on a VC-funded model, however pedestrian or deceptive the functionality or offering may be.

I will refrain from delving into this arena as it is outside the scope of this book.

A final thought.

If you must explain the meaning of your name to anyone, you have lost the cause.

How many thousands can you explain it to? The inability of that would eventually lead to wasteful and avoidable media spends. The fervour and anxiety to generate names only with memorability as the key can be a disaster if financial considerations are relevant.

I must repeat: If economic relevance doesn't find a place of importance, many aspects do not hold credence. That would be the route to valuation based on user acquisition and VC funding, irrespective of brand/value creation and legacy building. As I have outlined repeatedly, that is not in the purview of this book.

A young girl from my company's knowledge community of 'Diamonds in The Sky' (DITS), barely out of her teens but with a killer ambition to be the next unicorn, called in for some advice. She presented a couple of names for her start-up, looking for ratification for one of them.

I explained that she needed to consider the relevance of the business she was in and the audience she would be catering to, as these would be the driving factors to create a compelling name. But she continued to be persistent.

As I relented to her impatience, if only to acknowledge the urgency, I gave her an option.

Instantly she exclaimed, "But that doesn't sound like a *unicorn name*!"

Her response was shocking! I honestly could not believe what she said and had to make her repeat it to test my sanity. In the anxiety to become the fastest money and fame-making machine, at any cost, many seem to have forgotten the very core of what constitutes success. The fallacy in her thinking has origins in not understanding the following.

Amitabh Bachchan, Shahrukh Khan, Steve Jobs, Apple or Nike or even Swiggy, have not succeeded because of their name alone. However, the name has helped in their journey and has now attained prominence due to what the business or person has achieved.

Of late, many have taken the route of *services* to create success stories. The critical factor to note is that most also have origins in creating 'a first' in the market. Be it Dunzo, Paytm, Zomato or Ola. Even though a few were not the very first, they still were part of the unique *'first three'* in their category. As I mentioned earlier, that is a critical element to achieve the impossible, as even Google has proved. Though Yahoo was well entrenched in the genre of 'search', Google has gone on to become the undisputed leader. A strong reason was that the space was occupied by only one powerful brand, not *three*. This does not however lessen the credit of having created a far more technologically advanced product.

Additionally, in such high-repeat frequency services, *memorability* *a*nd verb convertibility (dunzoed or swiggied) play a significant role. As the first to offer solutions to a unique unsolved problem (Option 1 in Mantra 3), they had the luxury of not necessarily adhering to the other two elements of functionality and emotionality. However, adding these two factors could have cemented their place in the upper echelons far more.

Do This ACTION Exercise Now!

It is now that time again to review the name you are toying with for your new start-up.

If you currently have an ongoing business, analyse whether and how you can tune that name better to achieve all that has been spelt out here.

MANTRA 6

YOUR BABY'S UMBILICAL CORD TUGS HERE

How to Create a Game-Changing Tagline

"

Your tagline is the true lifeline of your business

The nurturing of a foetus, its very existence, is carried out through the umbilical cord from the mother.

In the business arena, too, there is a powerful umbilical cord that not just connects but serves as a conduit to transmit the company's vision to the hearts of its potential customers.

This essential element, recognised by the legends, is almost missing or not dealt with appropriately in most other companies.

Referred to by different names with subtle differences, such as tagline or company slogan, *this is the lifeline of any business.* Yes. It has the power to move mountains and establish a company as a true legend.

When Nike researched and came up with the globally acclaimed 'Just Do It,' it recognised it was not just creating a nice-sounding phrase but something much beyond that.

It was 6 a.m. in Osnabruck, a small town in Germany. Even inside the warmth of the hotel room, the outside temperature of -6° C was palpable.

As the alarm rang for my morning walk, it set off multiple thoughts.

"C'mon, you've done this for four successive days. You deserve a break."

"One day will not make a difference."

"Exercise alone does not contribute everything. You need rest too."

As I contemplated burrowing back into my blanket and taking in a couple more hours of that divine sleep, my eyes fell on the pair of shoes lying at the foot of the bed. The line pounded through my head: 'Just Do It.'

This message changed all my thoughts.

When one hears this line, it creates new neural pathways in the brain.

It makes one 'feel' like a decision-maker.

It makes one 'feel' like a winner.

Makes one 'feel' like an achiever.

Someone who can go beyond human boundaries and accomplish whatever they set out to do.

Within fifteen minutes, I was walking along that quaint path by the church, the exhilarating morning breeze stinging my face.

I stated earlier: ***Nike does not sell shoes.***

It is in the emotional business of creating formidable attitudes; it transforms the ordinary into the extraordinary.

The reason it commands a 10x premium for every shoe it puts on someone's feet.

In the world of unstoppable legends, all of them share this commonality.

They all understand the power and the impact of a tagline and possess the ability to create that magical lifeline which strikes emotional chords and penetrates deep into the customers' subconscious to ensure they come into the brand's fold.

Once again, the origin is fundamental. To reaffirm the emotional business in a manner that tugs at the heartstrings.

A well-structured, deeply thought-through tag(life)line precisely performs that.

This MANTRA is the exploration to create a game-changing tagline for your business.

Look at some of the top companies' immortal taglines (slogans).

The greatest from time immemorial:

NIKE

'Just Do It'

MASTERCARD

'There are some things money can't buy. For everything else, there's Mastercard'

SAMSUNG

'Do what you can't'

APPLE
'Think Different'

GILLETTE
'The Best a Man can Get'

COCA-COLA
'Open Happiness'

Every tagline is an emotional arrow aimed at inspiring the customers to go beyond themselves—tugging at their heartstrings to generate an emotional bond.

On the contrary, look at some slogans that shout down at us. At airports, malls and other places of high traffic and audience footfalls.

'India's best tile manufacturer'

'The Best Digital Services'

'The No.1 furniture company'

Spot the fundamental difference?
These companies are about themselves. What they do. How they are the best. How they know everything. *Merely loaded with features and benefits.* It is them talking about themselves.
But they miss one basic tenet.
Everyone can speak about themselves. It carries no credibility. And most importantly, they miss the biggest mantra. Of not recognising the critical differentiator. Of not connecting through the *emotional element* of the business. And that is precisely what the top organisations accomplish effortlessly.

Les Brown, regarded as the world's greatest motivational speaker says, "No one cares who you are, what you do. All they care about is what value is in it for them."

So how does one create the *perfect tagline*?

First and foremost, it should be driven by an emotional benefit. Simultaneously it should open up an avenue to encourage and ideally *empower the customer to take action.* Thereby giving rise to a sense of ownership in the product or service as well as a feeling of achievement. It is never about the brand and what it can do. It is only about what the customer should *feel* and *do* because of the emotional trigger the brand generates.

When this task is accomplished, to further lodge these commands effectively into the corridors of the brain, Al Ries, the late father of 'Brand Positioning', recommends four powerful methods.[1]

ALLITERATION

This is an *all-time great technique.*

Alliteration refers to having the same first letter in each word of a phrase.

For example, **Thums Up,** the popular Indian soft drink, has done wonders with its line

'Taste The Thunder'

The letter "T" is the first in all the words. This sequencing helps to forge a new neural pathway in the brain, thereby initiating an association between emotion and recall.

Jaguar has the same technique ingrained in its line,
'Don't Dream it. Drive It'

Intel, the B2B company, has taken this technique to exceptional heights. With its constant affirmation, *'Intel Inside'*, it achieves alliteration and emotion most powerfully.

And there is **Lexus** with *'The Passionate Pursuit of Perfection'*
A few other notable examples where alliteration has played a significant role even in *brand names* are *Coca-Cola, Bed Bath and Beyond, Hero Honda, Dunkin' Donuts, PayPal, Krispy Kreme, Best Buy* and *Range Rover.*
The late Al Ries further categorises wonderfully along a few more different paths.
The second tip for a great tagline is **RHYMING.**
A line that lends to powerful rhyming creates memorability that is essential to imprint the tagline in the brain's pathways. When fuelled with feeling (emotion), the line becomes invincible.

Look at some of the compelling taglines incorporating **rhyming.** Incidentally, notice this timeless proverb uses rhyming: *'An apple a day keeps the doctor away.'*

Timex
'Takes a licking and keeps on ticking'

'Beanz means Heinz' is a line that took **Heinz** on a heady path of success.
Rhyming is a very effective tool to embed something in the brain and propel memory along with recall.

It is not without reason that we remember our nursery poems so easily, even beyond their meaning (sometimes even the disquieting ones). These are lodged in our brain far more significantly than many of the greatest lessons we learn in the best universities simply because of the rhyme.

Next on the list, the late Ries recommends, is the strategy of a line with a dual meaning, the **DOUBLE ENTENDRE.**
The most powerful taglines in this category will always have a place in the immortal hall of fame.

De Beers
'*A Diamond is Forever*'
This line communicates not only the permanence of a diamond but also the relationship it connotes—stirring the heart most uniquely.
The duality in meaning combines the eternal nature of the stone and the long-sustaining relationship of love in a thoughtful manner.

Deere, the company that manufactures the best farm equipment, was the talk of the town when it produced the line that created history,
'*Nothing runs like a Deere*'

This tagline accentuates the functionality of the high performance of a Deere product and ensures the emotional element is integrated with it, thereby creating a memorability of incalculable value. It works exceptionally by using 'deer' as a pun for the fast-running animal and the brand name Deere.

Look at **Lays.**
'2 to 1, you can't eat just one'
This double entendre, coupled with rhyming, creates memorability based on the neurological pathways the two meanings offer, one of double the quantity and the other of a bet. This provides the required connection for the brain to safeguard this line in the annals of its memory cabinets.

Tag Heuer
The watch brand that set a new standard in toughness. And nothing could be more apt than relating its functionality to the owner's tenacity (emotionality) with the line, *'Don't crack under pressure'*

Look at the creatively crafted tagline of one of the most successful automotive companies, **Toyota.**
'Let's go places'

All these lines have been brilliantly woven around the dual connotations of the brand's performance, both functional and esoteric, with human emotional indulgence. For example, *'going places'* has the overtones of both success and extensive travel.

The last of what Ries calls the *'mental glue'* is **REPETITION.** The brain loves repetition. It is easy for words or phrases with repetition to penetrate the subconscious zone of the mind, something we will talk about in greater detail a little later.
Here are a few companies that have significantly succeeded in using this strategy.

FedEx does not say, 'When it has to be positively there'.

Its line is '*When it absolutely, positively has to be there overnight.*' It recognised the power of repetition; even today, most of its communication reinforces this.

McDonald's, which sells simple burgers and not necessarily the best in the field, uses this strategy to the hilt.
Look at some of its taglines over the years.[2]

'Love a Burger, Love a McDonald's'
'Bacon bacon bacon'
'Good food, good value'
'You want it, need it, you gotta have it'

These lines have evolved over the years and significant research has gone into the details of this repetition intricacy, whereby it has developed certain specific methodologies of word pattern formation to create the required memory penetration.[2] Such is the power of this method to keep memorability at the highest possible plane.

So, what exactly should the tagline do to achieve near perfection in results?
As explained earlier, beyond memorability, a tagline is most effective if it engages the customer's brain in a manner that propels and *empowers them to act* in the direction the company desires. This can happen if emotion is firmly entrenched so that it stirs the customer's neural pathways.

What exactly is the outcome when the above process is incorporated?

In the world of biochemistry, we realise that the neurons in our brain respond and react to one stimulus: Feeling. This is the word that separates the 'also ran' companies from the legends. The difference between people tied to the 'leash' of the business versus those with complete freedom and control over their lives. *The tagline (the umbilical cord of business) is the one, therefore, that transmutes the company philosophy through the hearts of the customer into action.* This drives the customer to take ownership of that action, ensuring its consummation.

I recently advised a company in the business of providing CAD (Computer-Aided Design) solutions. The challenge for this B2B company was identifying the right emotion and then translating it into the perfect tagline that tugs at the heartstrings. Numerous iterations led to the conclusion that the emotional benefit the company offered was *freedom* to the end-user, the advantage of being able to utilise 'saved time' from incorporating their software.

The first option we conceived was 'Creating freedom for you.' But this tagline had one fundamental flaw. It talked about '*us*' and how '*we*' do it for you. It lacked both credibility and empowerment.

As we spoke earlier, the tagline must make the customer's heart beat faster and instil the 'feeling' to act.

The messianic line 'Just Do It' will always show you the way whenever you are stuck in the journey of designing an all-powerful tagline.

Thus, we went back to the drawing board to look for that statement that would *make the customer feel 'they have achieved something'*. A message that could generate the flow of feel-good chemicals — dopamine and oxytocin (emanating out of love for oneself). That, in turn, will trigger the customer to feel empowered and act in a manner which is emotionally related to your product.

The line we finally arrived at was:

'Rediscover Your Freedom'

This achieves three objectives.

i) Subtly conveys that the customer has lost his freedom.
ii) It communicates the positive element that all is not lost. That the customer can still '*rediscover* that lost freedom'. And we, the company, will be the facilitators.
iii) Most importantly, it transfers the power of action to the customers, empowering them as the evaluator of benefits.

Summary:

The perfect tagline is evolved when you create an emotive stir in the customers' hearts/minds and **make them act** and take ownership of that action.

It must bring together the following ingredients.

1. It should have nothing to do with what the company does, be it self-glorification or description of services provided.
2. It should emphasise what *the customer should do*, **not** what the company does.
3. It should be highly driven on an emotive front.

4. It should ideally follow one or more of the principles the late Al Ries recommended.

Disclaimer:

In case the tagline can perform such a decisive action of empowering and mobilising the customer, which is the main objective, it could even bypass the standard principles of tagline creation.

Do This ACTION Exercise Now!

Do you have a powerful tagline for your business? If yes, run it through the crucible of the above parameters and ensure it lives up to them.

If not, create one right away with all the techniques prescribed. It will save your life one day!

MANTRA 7

THE NEW A.R.T ON THE CANVAS

The 80/20/80 Formula for Customer Base Explosion

> *It is seven times more difficult to generate business from a new customer than from an existing one!*

In the post-Covid era, this would be the most noticeable action of most companies: '*Chasing new customers*'.

Since many businesses have shrunk and customer psychology in buying patterns has changed, a majority of companies are spending most, if not all, of their time chasing new ones. The word for this is **ACQUISITION**, the A of A.R.T. that we will discuss more in detail in this chapter.

This shifts the focus away from not only other projects but also the all-important, existing customer, creating the '**Reverse or Inverted Funnel' effect.**

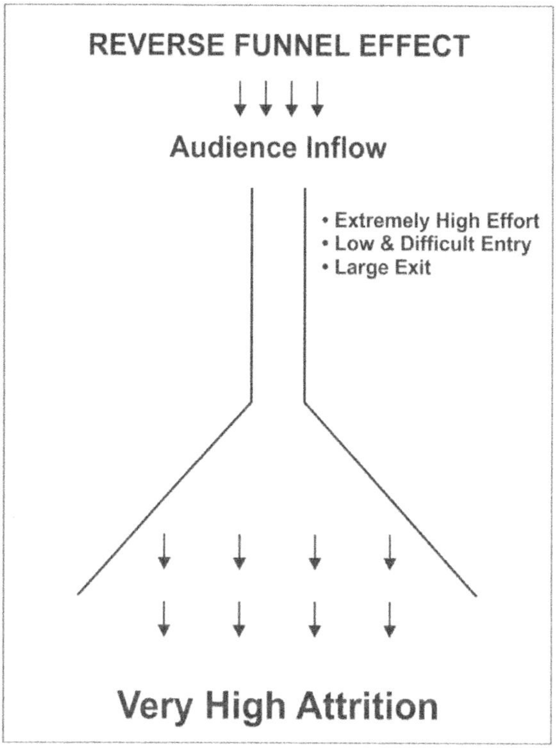

In this effect, with prolonged and intense effort, the new customers are drawn in a crowded manner through the narrow stem, but soon they scatter away like flies. And the struggle continues, keeping you on a treadmill of activity you can never get out of!

This MANTRA, therefore, is about viewing the customers through an entirely new lens.

Scene: Breakfast time, a luxury hotel in Chennai. As my eyes searched for an empty table, I spotted a space across from a single gentleman, after whose consent I sat down.

Soon we began to exchange pleasantries which led me to ask him what his work involved. He took great pleasure in telling me about his business, his hundreds of customers, his turnover base and all his offices across the country.

I was thoroughly impressed.

I then queried what would happen if he took a two-month vacation. Would his business grow or be the same?

He nearly choked on his food.

He exclaimed, "Two months? I cannot leave even for two days. Even if I do, it would be a big challenge if the internet is unavailable."

Wow! Not sure if I sensed pride in this, but I let it pass.

When all your work makes you a dog on the leash with no freedom to pursue what you truly desire, apart from the business you drive, it may be time to ask this critical question.

"Am I doing what I am doing truly towards the **WHY** *I am doing or am I performing a ritual towards an imaginary tomorrow, where I wake up one day to find that I have not just missed smelling the roses but let my whole life go by?"*

How often have we not witnessed even large company owners wanting to know the exact monthly canteen bill or tracking the sales of a specific product in a small territory?

No, this is not passion or commitment. It is an obsession. An inability to let go of the reins and wield power in the guise of passion.

True power lies in channelising a set of forces, each of which, while moving an inch, slowly moves a mountain. Which you, on your own, would not even have been able to conceive.

The A.R.T. funnel

We saw how the 'Reverse Funnel' effect takes your 'steam' away while trying to keep the business afloat.

What if we were to upturn that funnel in a way that a vast majority of customers come in, but only a few get drained through the narrow stem while the others stay? This image would define the A.R.T funnel.

In this scenario, most customers who come into the fold stay for far longer durations.

The potential dropouts are persuaded to stay on with the offer of multiple incentives, leaving only a final few to exit the funnel through the all-difficult narrow stem.

This process is the **'R'** of A.R.T—**RETENTION.**

Why is retention so important? 'RETENTION' is that incredible power that repeatedly makes the customer return to your brand. The power that enhances penetration and engagement, not for a short duration but for the entire customer lifetime, generating invaluable Customer Lifetime Value (CLV).

Customer Lifetime Value

What is customer lifetime value (CLV)? Let us explore the calculation of CLV and how it funnels exponential growth for a company.

Assume a customer purchases a product or a service unit at a price of 'x' once a month. This would make his contribution to the company 12x in one year. If he remains a user for 15 years, during this period his revenue towards the company would be 180x.

Even if their visits to your brand get reduced to once every two months, reducing your revenue by 50 per cent and lowering it to 90x, it would be a far better option than someone who buys your brand at double your price, i.e., 2x, but stays only for a couple of usage cycles.

This analysis forms the fundamental tenet that establishes retention as the key to building a long-term, sustainable business that has the potential to grow into a legend.

Over a 100 years ago, the Pareto Principle pointed to an incredible insight – that 80 per cent of business is generated by 20 per cent of customers.

Further, the finding that a new customer is seven times more difficult to command business from only adds to the reason this twenty per cent must be treated with reverence.

Ironically, today, most companies spend over 80 per cent of their time acquiring new customers but almost negligible time on the existing ones on whom their very existence depends, taking them for granted. They thus sound their own death knell.

So, in our company we have established a formula wherein twice a week, i.e., 40 per cent of the available time, employees must spend 80 per cent of working hours catering to the 20 per cent of customers who generate 80 per cent of the business.

This formula, while being an extension of Pareto's Principle, cuts the diffusion on effectively retaining the customers in our fold to maximise the CLV.

Do This ACTION Exercise Now!
Create the CLV map for your top customers, relate it to the time you devote to each of them and ask if it makes you feel satisfied. If not, change the matrix immediately.

Finally, the **'T'** of A.R.T—**TRANSFERENCE**

This is the fastest road to that elusive 'freedom'. When the customer takes on the role of 'the silent salesman', it paves the way for releasing the strong disconnect between what you 'want' to do and what you 'have' to do. It makes way from the mundane to the sublime.[1]
It provides you opportunities towards more meaningful goals and passion, rather than having to be tied to what you do as a grind.
Remember, you do not want to be that breakfast-table-business-owner in Chennai whose neck is tied to an 'invisible' leash.

Creating ambassadors (not the paid celebrity type) who buy into your vision and are the true patrons of your products is the perfect way to freedom wherein you can be released from that leash. Indeed, you do not want to be entirely disconnected from that leash and lose ownership. But extending the connecting cord and ensuring the business is being looked after by someone who cares provides the moment of freedom.

That is what **TRANSFERENCE** does.
It transfers the burden of new customer acquisition onto existing customers. This is how the A.R.T effect comes into force through creating the **A.R.T funnel, the 'Upturned Funnel'**, in contrast to the 'Reverse Funnel' effect.

What, then, is this **'A.R.T funnel'** and how can that be influenced towards exponentially changing the fortunes of companies?

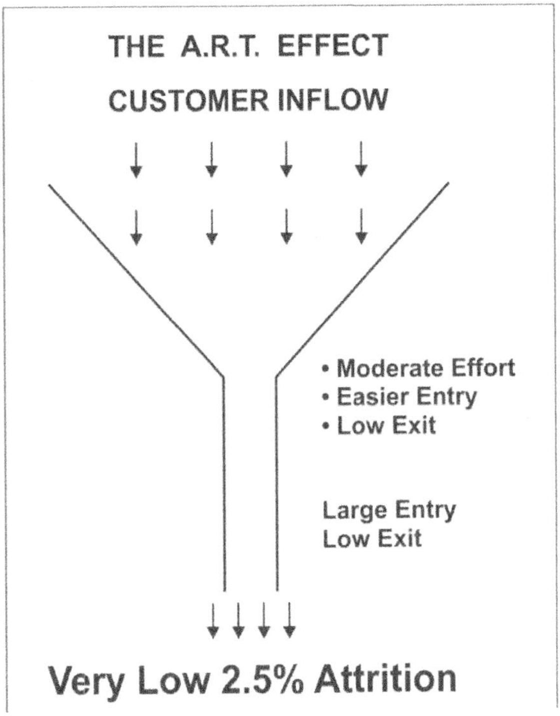

The A.R.T effect thus brings on the crowd flow at the acquisition stage, as earlier, but with significant retention at every point of slippage with the final drop-offs at a meagre percentage (approximately 2.5 per cent, based on our internal research). Again, this is purely due to the powers of retention and transference, ensuring most of the customer base either constantly returns or scripting an entirely innovative customer acquisition strategy through existing customers.

Note: This conceptualisation of the 'Funnel Effect' needs to be looked at figuratively rather than literally. Since in a literal sense, everything would exit from a funnel one day.

In this analogy, the accumulated customers from the top of the funnel would be regularly moved into the jar of the customer database. In the above configuration of the A.R.T. funnel, the time available to move would be far greater than in the earlier case of the Reverse Funnel, thereby providing a large opportunity to fill the jar substantially.

One of the most effective ways of generating and enhancing this A.R.T effect is through the RPF-SPF model we have designed in our company.

THE RPF-SPF MODEL

I have always been fascinated and influenced by the powerful Boston Consulting Group (BCG) model, which focuses on the meeting points and quadrants of market growth and relative market share.

After analysing multiple successful companies that built *customer ambassadors,* we created a model based on the two factors of RPF and SPF, *Revenue Protection Factor and Stickiness Protection Factor.*
In simple terms, this model integrates **revenue** and another critical factor, **stickiness,** which deals with how the customer 'sticks' with the company, what the driving forces are and how to nurture them better.

Most business owners are in chase mode when it comes to revenue. Revenue is constantly in front of them but still eluding them. The need, therefore, is to create an avenue where revenue is not an illusory object that is being 'chased' after but is evolved, i.e., a by-product.
Hence, the key is to delight the customers, so that they not only return but also recommend your product to others.

The following diagram illustrates the modus operandi.

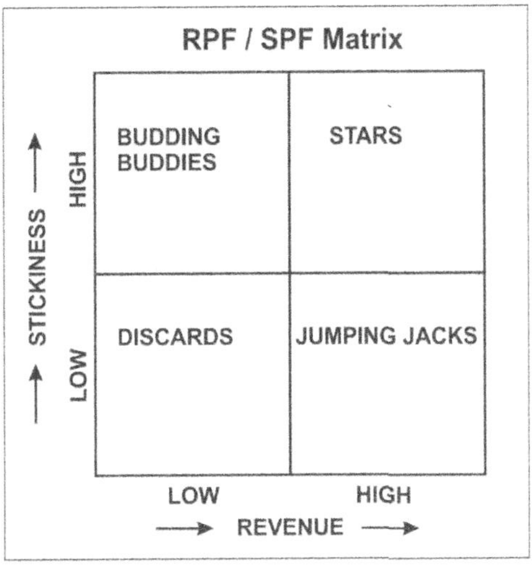

This representation is a simple four-quadrant model that derives its importance based on two critical factors: customer revenue and customer stickiness. Stickiness, defined as repeat visits of a customer to the brand in at least three of the four subsequent purchases, is a level ahead of loyalty.

Let us review each quadrant and the action strategies for them.

Quadrant 1 *(high-revenue, high-stickiness customers)*
These are undoubtedly the company's 'Stars' and the golden boys and girls. They generate increased revenue and also are exceptionally loyal. These customers need to be respected and nurtured with reverence. Unfortunately, most companies take them for granted and pay a considerable price. It is crucial to reaffirm genuine care and make them 'feel special' constantly.

For example, you could create a VIP group, felicitating them for their achievements, giving them first preference for a new product or company update or involve them in an upcoming innovation, as you will learn in a later chapter. In addition, you could feature them in your important communications. The sign-off is 'making them feel special' and constantly being in touch with them.

Quadrant 2 *(high revenue, low stickiness)*
These are the 'Jumping Jacks'. They are customers who are high spenders but jump from brand to brand.

Conduct studies on the psychological factors that make them 'brand hoppers' and address them.

They could be eternally seeking change, newness, variety or greater value for money. Assess this and ensure they are catered to effectively.

Some simple but time-tested methods are where you engage with them for long-term commitment by luring them with both price and value advantages or creating loyalty groups where, yet again, the customers in the group are made to feel special.

Quadrant 3 *(low revenue, high stickiness)*

These are the 'Budding Buddies'. They are the buds of today, who will bloom tomorrow. They will be with you, provided you do not squander them away with your negligence. They see your vision and want to be a part of that. Ensure you treat them no differently from those in Quadrant 1.

One of the biggest mistakes that companies and individuals make is not giving importance to clients with low revenue salience. That can often be fatal. Not only do you lose the opportunity for future revenue, but they also become the 'demon ambassadors' and can be hugely detrimental. According to Esteban Kolsky, Former Research Director, Gartner, if a customer is not happy, 13% of them will share with 15 others or even more.

Quadrant 4 *(low revenue, low stickiness)*

These would require enormous time, effort and monetary considerations so they are best disregarded for any action. Being just a silent caterer to their occasional needs without risking them turning into demon ambassadors would be the perfect strategy for this quadrant audience.

These are the 'Discards'. Consider even dropping them if you have to and move on.

SUMMARY:

To establish freedom, you must create brand ambassadors who believe in your vision and are part of your troupe. And who better than your customers? Transference is that process that performs this enviable task of creating customer ambassadors so that you drive a vehicle of freedom.

Do This ACTION Exercise Now!

Create the RPF-SPF matrix for the top 80 per cent of your customers and map them on each quadrant. Create specific strategies for each customer group based on the action items described in the quadrants.

MANTRA 8

HOW WIDE CAN YOU CAST YOUR BUSINESS FISHING NET?

Novel Ways to Catapult Your Audience Size

> *"The weight of your fulfilment depends on how wide you cast your nets"-Israelmore Ayivor*

Changing the 'HOW' while keeping the 'What' and 'Why' unchanged

There comes a time when you feel you have reached a point where any further pushing will not generate incremental results from either the products or the services you provide. It is then that you need to step back and revisit the drawing board and the fundamental business matrix.

This chapter reveals the MANTRA to create new and expanded business enhancement dimensions for that matrix which focuses on two parameters.

Your audience

AND

Your products/services range.

With the obvious four quadrants:

1. *Current Products/Current Audience*
2. *Current Products/New Audience*
3. *New Products/Current Audience, and*
4. *New Products/New Audience*

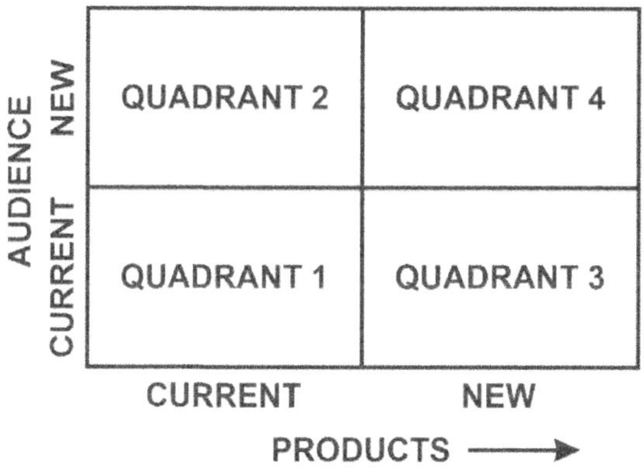

Effectively, the first space that gets exhausted or stops yielding incremental results is Quadrant 1 *(Current Products with the Current Audience)* for multiple reasons, namely, fatigue, penetration saturation, change in market scenarios in terms of excessive competition and a few other factors. Rather than be surprised when that occurs, you can be prepared with options that have credence in the other quadrants.

Start with the opening question again.

What emotional business are you in and what problems do your products or services aim to solve? Within that same framework, what ELSE can your business achieve or could you make it generate?

Let us look at what **Dunzo**, the now famous delivery service company, undertook when faced with such a situation in Covid. Dunzo suddenly felt the heat of a complete lockdown during Covid and went through an internal brainstorming of its core offering and core strengths. While recognising that its core offering was in the delivery service between two entities and having realised its original business had become unviable in that scenario, it pivoted around the same value offering into a one-way delivery service for medicines and critical food items. While the competition did exist from Swiggy and Zomato, it did not deter Dunzo for two reasons. One, the opportunity was significant and two, it was adhering to its core emotional business of trust and their value proposition of care.

This is a typical example of how you could create New Audience for the Current Product i.e., Quadrant 2.
If your offering is around service and the operating mechanism is geared to that and does not conflict with your main domain expertise, you have a winner.
Occasionally, solutions for new avenues emerge from the customers themselves and absolve you of the travails of figuring it out.

One such instance was when a team I was part of at **Sanyo Electronics**, Dubai, faced a perplexing scenario in the boardroom. In a small hamlet in one of the Emirates of the UAE, sales of a new 'baby washer' that had been launched recently reached record levels.

This oddity was puzzling, especially as there had been no significant promotion or effort in that region, nor had a cracker sales team been in place.

We drove along dusty roads to the interiors and reached that hamlet. We met one of the retailers and eagerly asked why the baby washer sales in that hamlet were outdoing sales elsewhere, more so when most customers did not fit the affordability or demographic consistency profile.

What he told us was something that we had not imagined in our wildest dreams and left us wholly bewildered.

He said the baby washer was being used not to wash small quantities of clothes as we had intended but as … hold your breath … a 'buttermilk churner'.

While this is an extreme example, it indicates how innovation and creativity can come to the fore to generate options beyond one's imagination.

This analogy is yet another instance of how new uses and, thereby, users (audience) can be created for the same product. *Once again, 'Quadrant 2' of 'Current Product/New Audience'.*

Instagram

We are very familiar with the core strengths with which Instagram has become the success story it is today— innovation and ability to capture millions worldwide with its offering.

Even Instagram, at some point, when faced with stagnancy, re-evaluated its portfolio and recognised an opportunity to consider newer offerings to the same audience.

Although it resembled Snapchat, launching the 'Stories' feature added novelty and an element of privacy as they would disappear after 24 hours. This new creation not only enhanced its user base but went streets ahead of Snapchat even in that similar space.

Yet another success story in the 'Quadrant 3' space of *New Products/Current Audience.*

Johnson & Johnson

On a few occasions, these innovations can pave the way for something significant in the current audience scenario itself. Johnson & Johnson discovered this in a hunt for the reason behind the magical sales boom of Johnson's baby soap in Thailand, a small country with little to offer in the demographic space of the product. The company found that since it was gentle on the skin, it was being extensively used in massage parlours, a complete incongruity.

While discovering this quadrant of *New Audience* for the *Current Product*, J&J hit upon the idea of highlighting an equivalent range of products for the adult segment, offering the promise of skin akin to babies through the promise of Johnson's baby lotion.

This discovery brought into the fold a '*New Audience*' of adults with the '*Current Product*' without even creating one. *It's a brilliant 'Quadrant 2' example.*

Whenever there is stagnation, ask yourself these two questions again:

1. What is my core emotional offering?
2. Why do customers prefer my product over others'?

Vicks Cough Drops

Late in the '70s, Vicks Cough drops (VCD) exhibited a slight stagnant curve. Detailed research revealed that while the product was used to relieve throat irritation, it was also used as an excellent mouth freshener and sometimes as an oral gratifier, like chewing gum. The challenge was that it was positioned as a 'cough reliever', which limited its perception as a product for someone under the weather.

Thereafter P&G shifted its focus to promoting the product as '*Vicks ki goli*' (Vicks drop). Here, with limited emphasis on the cough aspect, it addressed the oral gratification route while retaining the irritation-relieving element of the throat through the '*khich khich door karo*' ('relieve the irritation') tagline.

This re-positioning achieved something revolutionary as the size of the resultant new audience was now multiple times the size of the original one.

Yet again, a unique way and example of

How one can cater to a 'New Audience' with the 'Current Product' -Quadrant 2.

Amazon was and continues to be a great example of creating *New Uses/Products for its Current Audience (Quadrant 3).* It effectively masterminded this when it transitioned from 'only books' (product current at that time) to all other products,

of every kind, from the smallest to the largest. This offering generated an entirely uncharted avenue of *new products for the Current Audience (Quadrant 3)*. This action indirectly was also helpful in creating a *New Audience for the Current Product* (books and their platform). i.e., Quadrant 2.
Amazon, recognising its stagnation and inability to move beyond a particular level, was exceptionally successful at this innovation. History has proven that these innovations have transformed the brand value to unimaginable levels, only because it could leverage its captive audience with an entire range of new options without losing focus of its value proposition and being in line with its vision.

Amazon then integrated these changes with other value additions of speed, convenience and service. That's why Amazon rules the world, having navigated skilfully through *both Current Products/New Audience of Quadrant 2 and New Products/Current Audience of Quadrant 3.*

Quadrant 4 of New Products to a *New Audience* would be an elaborate and tedious journey which is almost a replication of venturing into a completely new start-up. That could be an independent vertical in a company or evaluated when all the options mentioned above have been exhausted.

Do This ACTION Exercise Now!
Generate at least *one 'New Audience'* base for your current set of products which has the potential to expand your product usage and, thereby, revenues, substantially.

MANTRA 9

THINKING AT THE EDGE OF THE BOX

Design Thinking

(Co-creation)

> *"I have always found that you must work with the customer experience first and then work backwards to the technology. You cannot start with the technology first and later figure out what to sell."–Steve Jobs.*

This chapter now unveils yet another powerful MANTRA to extend and expand the customer base.

When soap companies were screaming from the billboards about how beautiful a woman looks after using their products, in an unprecedented manner **DOVE** decided to attempt something incredibly different.

Dove realised that apart from the audience seeking physical beauty, a vast segment felt ignored because of their looks or, rather, the lack of them. And no number of shining beauties beaming away on television would change that.

So, the brand invited women from across various strata and conducted an experiment. Each woman was asked to sit in a studio with a skilled artist who would sketch her image - with one difference: He would not be seeing them. Instead, he would draw solely based on the 'perceptions' of the woman's own description of her physical attributes. If she were to describe her nose as short or long, their mouth as curved or broad or their chin or hair in a particular manner, he would create the sketch accordingly. The women would then leave. Dove would then repeat this experiment with another variation.

This time around, a friend of the woman who participated in the earlier experiment would be invited to describe her friend's features.

The subject would then be presented with both sketches, one based on how she described herself and the other one based on her friend's description of her.

The results were simply astonishing.

The sketches based on the self-descriptions, especially of those who perceived themselves as not so physically attractive, were in line with their personal perceptions. But the perception of the friend's description revealed a completely different person – because they went beyond just the physical aspects.

Sometimes they showed a caring whisper near the eye, an all-pervading calmness in the face, a radiance or an underlying energy. These observations resulted in sketches that were far more beautiful than the ones based on the subject's description of herself.

The results of this unique experiment enabled Dove to achieve what in today's parlance is known as design thinking or co-creation.

This involves bringing the audience into the fold and providing them with a unique platform that makes them feel good about themselves. Dove created a new emotional business through the co-creation of 'Real Beauty'[1], which sought to assert that beauty went far beyond physical characteristics and connoted something more holistic, thus 'creating' an entirely new audience.

'Real Beauty' was now defined as confidence, power, empathy, one that had boundaries only in the infinite. This redefining of the concept of beauty not only elevated Dove's image as a brand that 'cared' for women but also expanded its user base by several multiples and brought into its ken a completely unaddressed audience which would have perceived Dove as yet another product for the 'conventionally beautiful'.

The emotion that Dove created, which was unique, was *self-worth*. It was now in the emotional business of enhancing the self-esteem of women.

This is CO-CREATION: Created by the brand, along with its audience.

When your business needs to scale to new levels, but you are drawing a blank, this is a powerful weapon to bring to the fore.

This MANTRA helps you break barriers and forge ahead into zones less travelled.

The only prerequisite: Deep-dive reflection.

LAYS

When you have run out of options for products and growth, the ideal route is to involve your customer in the strategy process directly. Interestingly, that is what Lays, the potato chip brand, did.

When Lays came to a bend in the road and wanted to scale up growth, it hit upon the famous *'Do Us A Flavour'* strategy. In an unconventional first-time approach, Pepsi, the parent company of Lays, invited customers to recommend a flavour.

The flavour chosen would not just be manufactured but also have the person's name and picture on the pack. That is true co-creation involving customers in an aspect crucial to the brand.

This customer engagement combined the emotions of enhancing self-worth and aspiration, energising the customer to invest in the brand, thus incorporating a whole new audience base. This activity also communicated the brand's values and showed that they cared and genuinely. About what the customer believed in.

A new page in the history of customer engagement was written that day.

Go and meet the customer. Engage with them. Listen to the voice of magic.

As Gurcharan Das, former Chairman of P&G, India, had said about going to the market when he discovered a new usage of Vicks VapoRub (the practice of adding a spoonful of Vicks VapoRub to a bowl of boiling water to infuse the steam with the drug): *"You will be surprised at the patterns of customer behaviour that no amount of thought and testing at your end would have shown the possibility of its existence."*

One of the most important reasons why companies like **PROCTER & GAMBLE** not just survive but overcome and dominate the market for decades is this unique approach: It has an unwavering belief in the value of market research, to the exclusion of any personal preference, however high up the ladder it is expressed.

That is what separates the legends from the ordinary.

How about the story of a $1 billion revenue product that initially was a complete write-off? Here is a success story of P&G achieved by incorporating the consumer as a partner.

Probably P&G missed the golden words of Steve Jobs quoted at the beginning of this chapter or was out of time. Whatever the reason, when it accidentally created a product that, sprayed on any object, would remove a bad odour, it was so excited that it introduced this brand as Febreze in the market, hoping to find the customer later.

Febreze was positioned to drive away smells of household pets from pet owners' homes and was launched with all possible fanfare. Instead, it ended as a miserable flop, with stocks piling up on all the retailers' shelves.

Come market research data and voila! It revealed that the answer to the fundamental question of what-emotional-business-are-we-in had gone missing.

The owners, who were emotionally connected to their pets, never found their pets' smell offensive. Those who did not own pets could not relate to this phenomenon.

Another emotive imbalance: The pet parent customer also felt judged and blamed as the product seemed to imply that they were not keeping their homes clean enough.

But P&G is not a legend without reason. It did not just feel sorry for itself, pack up its bags and leave. Instead, it conducted research among the consumers who continued to use the product. What made them buy it even as hundreds had turned into non-users?

(Chip and Dan Heath use the term 'Bright Spot' in their book *Switch* for such findings.)

To P&G's amazement, one of the 'users' was a woman who used Febreze on her clothes after she cleaned the rooms as a final step in her cleaning ritual. This finding led to the discovery of multiple customers using the product not to 'get rid of a smell' but as a positive way to conclude something. *"P&G team realized that 'Febreze' need not be a pain killer (for removing bad smells), but could be a vitamin (not solving pain, but providing energy-boosting the visceral experience)"*[2]

P&G then added a special perfume to Febreze that was in sync with the customer's needs and co-created a product where the outcome could be observed through the perfume smell. This would almost be a subtle communication to others of their sense of cleanliness. The pleasant smell at the end bringing a sense of relaxation and pride. Over a period, the smell was the finality that a job was well completed and this slowly over time became a habit. Biochemistry again comes into play as dopamine (the feel-good chemical) gets released when we feel a job is well done, thus creating a habit in the customer's mind to repeat the act. This ritual effectively ensures that 'stickiness' is continued.

When a business either comes to a halt or is on a stagnant path, making the customer a partner and creating an entity that aligns with their needs is a brilliant co-creation methodology, as legends constantly demonstrate.

IKEA and **LEGO** are two other famous companies that engage in co-creation constantly.

Look at IKEA's core values. They include togetherness, simplicity and caring for people and the planet[3].

Togetherness stands tall in its values. As a result, IKEA constantly conducts programs involving the customers in recommending solutions for problems the customers face and generating new innovative ideas.

Similarly, at LEGO, customers can be partners in the company's future ideas and execution through continuous engagement.

Having seen the potential of co-creation, let us now explore how this process can be put into action and implemented successfully.

How do you co-create?

To summarise, co-creation is not a feedback mechanism. It is way beyond that, both in scope and results. It is a collaborative 'New Product Development Initiative' where consumers are invited to contribute and/or select the content of a new product offering from a basket of options presented by the company[4].

The organisation then markets the 'selected' products and services.

Amazon Prime is a splendid example where employees successfully incorporated co-creation, contributing to the massive expansion of its outreach and enabling the company to reach unimaginable heights.

A few essential techniques for effective co-creation:

1. Define the exact need or objectives of why you want to co-create.
2. Identify the clear niche of the target audience.
3. Create a defined engagement platform and methodology to interact with the customers.
4. Provide value. This is crucial. The customer needs to see clear and measurable value. This value need not be financial, though that could be a great fillip. It could be psychological, where, for instance, the customer is given visibility on social media for his contribution.

   Starbucks has an effective process of co-creation wherein it uploads on social media the idea along with the picture of the individual who contributed it. It realises the importance of the emotional value of self-worth and uses co-creation as a tool to enhance it constantly.

   If you are a small company, you may not be able to provide substantial instant financial value. But you could link it to the product's success and share the profits from the new development, which would then be a very effective method to enrol the customer into an ownership model.

5. Clearly communicate the methodology and be highly transparent in the selection process. This could make or break this whole project.
   Lays smartly empowered the customer to be the judge and choose the best flavour in its co-creation project of *Do Us A Flavour* rather than spend considerable money and time deciding the winner.

The advantages of co-creation cannot be overemphasised.

* It spares you from the pressure of being at a dead-end regarding revenues and profits, pushing the same products to the same audience. Generates radically new ways to create excitement among your audience.
* Enhances 'stickiness' (covered in *'Mantra' 7* on RPF/SPF) whereby the *loyalty factor* is multiplied manifold.
* There can be no better way to generate customer ambassadors than to have them take complete ownership of the product's success.

Do This ACTION Exercise Now!

For every product or service you currently oversee, identify an opportunity where you can involve the customer and co-create a product or service that can generate unique value and scale up your business. Ensure you follow all the steps outlined earlier in this chapter.

MANTRA 10

SHOW ME THE MONEY

Cash Is King? The World of Funding

> *"Money is only a tool. It will take you wherever you wish, but it will not replace you as the driver."–Ayn Rand*

The oxygen of the world. And in the world of business, it takes on an esoteric meaning. MONEY. So, what is the secret of the money MANTRA?

The bank was bustling with customers. A long weekend was around the corner. At the far end of the corner office, the bank manager was deeply buried in the glowing screen of the computer. He probably had a presentation for which he had few answers. His forehead looked furrowed.

This meeting with the bank manager was important. We had nearly run out of money for the start-up I was heading. With orders aplenty in the bag, it shouldn't be difficult to get a sign-off on the $2-million debt we were seeking. Or so I thought.

He did not seem too pleased to be taken away from the numbers on the screen, but he was a friend. He knew I would not bother him unless I had a specific purpose. I was visiting him, my CFO and CMO in tow.

I went through the well-rehearsed narrative of how the mobile phone market was poised for a boom and how our software had innovative fixes that could alter the landscape of the entire industry. He listened patiently, waiting for my final push.

I also ensured him that many top telecom organisations had given us orders and that soon, we would begin our ascent to the top.

He calmly questioned, "So what's the problem, Vijay?"

I then explained to him that to be able to fulfil the orders that would take us to that top, we would require a loan of $2 million. He did not bat an eyelid. Two million dollars was less than the interest the bank would earn on the disbursed loans in a week. This was chicken feed. So, I was reasonably sure we would be walking out of the office with the paper of commitment.

In the same calm manner, he said, "Vijay, that may not be possible."

We were pretty taken aback. As I started my spiel all over again, he stopped me and said, "We won't be able to inject funds as debt into areas where there is no long-term certainty for business. With no collateral to support, it would be a complete non-starter."

We were in shock. But that day, I understood one important principle. In the funding world, debt would not be the fodder available if you are dabbling in technology, software and services to create future-based products, even if it is an orange moon. That would be the road taken by companies who generate constant revenues with a proven track record as their products get rolled out with receivables and other definite repayment sources as a fallback. In contrast, working capital (the capital of a business used in its day-to-day trading operations, i.e., current assets minus the current liabilities or in short, the money available to meet your current, short-term obligations) can be serviced by debt.

What, then, are other avenues for funding when you are speeding on the highway of product innovations with prospects of certain success but whose fruits will only be realised in the distant future?

This MANTRA will unveil a few of those options.

The buzzword of today: Venture Capital (VC) funding. Entities that buy into your equity for a mutually agreed price in return for a stake in your company.

In this world of VC funding, as you find yourself in the rail station of entrepreneurship, two questions will face you.

The first is '*which*' train to board that will take you to the correct destination, connoting the type of VC that you should even consider.

The second is '*when*' to board the VC train, having identified the correct train. Implying when to engage with a VC. Recognising the venture capitalists' objectives and what drives them will be the critical factor that can provide solutions to the above questions. Let us pause and take a detour to understand what business the VCs are in.

Like you, the VCs, too, are on a serious business journey. They are entities that have garnered funds from private investors who want to see exceptionally high returns in a relatively short period. It could be in the vicinity of thirty percent IRR (Internal Rate of Return) within three to five years.

They also are, many a time, constrained by the period during which they necessarily have to invest those funds. This restriction, in turn leads to a situation wherein, if one particular year has cyclical disadvantages (for example, Covid) and they have a three-year objective, they are forced to invest in the remaining two years. This would then shift their IRR gears substantially and, along with that, their objectives.

This also means that VCs move into investing with the necessary condition of an 'exit' plan, at least the majority of them.

What, then, does this entail for you as an entrepreneur?

We return to the original question we posed at the beginning and the very purpose of this book.

***Why** do you want to do **what** you want to do?*

If that 'why' relates to the short-term wealth creation mechanism, it goes beyond the purview of this book, whose sole purpose is to bring forward the legend in people like you, whose supremacy endures for decades and probably centuries.

Thus, you can see that sometimes you and the VC who invests in you could have highly conflicting objectives. The outcome of that can only head in one direction: friction and stress. Not exactly the reasons for your entrepreneurial exploration!

What you are seeking in your expedition to legendary status is 'patience capital' along with financial infusion. Identifying someone who resonates with your objectives would answer the question of *which VC train to board.*

Effectively the answer to the question of *when* to board the VC train is based on what, in engineering terms, is called an 'impedance match.'

An example of an impedance mismatch is when a school marching band cannot participate in a parade because it cannot afford the cost of fuel for the bus.

Essentially, anyone who can obstruct your flow (impedance) will not be anywhere close to the ideal match/fit for you as an investor.

But a great match is when the financial infusion is at a stage where every penny of the capital propels a new and incremental rate of revenues and possible profits. This situation arises when the company's growth rate is far greater than the sustainable growth rate (the rate at which it took on the initial period of business evolution without external fund infusion) and could be a great place to start accepting external funds. That would be an ideal impedance match.

On the other hand, there could be markets of astronomical proportions that could yield what are termed as 'blitz' growth rates, where there is an urgency to acquire market share at any cost – what we see happening today where profit discussion is thrown out of the window, almost as if it is an unholy word.

This urgency could be a dangerous route for the entrepreneur, especially if your objective is sustained value creation to play the game of legends. Though this could be an exciting game for the VCs who could pass off the high, unsustainable growth rates as business sustenance in the quest for another hungry but less savvy investor, it certainly could be a death knell for the business owner.

But not everyone can afford the luxury of waiting eternally without any external financial inflows. Cash is oxygen for a start-up and continues to be for every business. There will come the point sometimes when you must make some difficult choices.

Suppose you have absolutely no option and are at the crossroads of giving up entirely versus submitting yourself to the situation of having to accept funds from the investor/VC whose objectives clearly conflict with yours. In that case, you can resort to the 'postponement strategy'. You can embark on the VC train with one understanding — over the coming few years, you can ride this train only to disembark a little later to board the train of another VC whose vision matches yours. As a last resort, at some point, you can even press the Abort button. Nothing can be more harmful than embarking on a voyage where there is constant interference from an investor whose objectives are irreconcilable with yours. I know such entrepreneurs who, having submitted to the dilution process repeatedly, have been haunted constantly by questions relating to the VC's agenda but are not even on the horizon of the entrepreneurs' vision. This unproductive interference occasionally leads to a schism and easing out of the entrepreneurs, with negligible returns from the very baby they had envisioned and created.

Now comes the billion-dollar question.

How much to dilute and at what price?

Frankly, the valuation game is more like who is calling whose bluff better. The earlier you dilute, the greater your chance of losing out on this game. You must build your own 'patience capital' and dilute only when it is genuinely not in the realm of possibility to continue.

The agenda could often be driven by VCs who seek to use your company as their 'exit strategy' as mentioned earlier.

The longer you constantly focus on the 'value creation' aspect for the customer, the smoother you will sail in safe waters.

There are various theories on the percentage to be diluted, but that, in my opinion, is driven by the nature of the business, its 'relevance quotient' in the marketplace over time and your personal aspirations.

And here is some heart-warming news. Certainly not the majority, but it comes as no surprise to witness unique businesses turning over billions of dollars that haven't stretched their hands to seek or subjugate themselves to financial behemoths.

Finally, it may be pertinent, yet ironic, to note that many view an initial public offering (IPO) as a route to seek funds from retail investors. Nothing could be farther from the truth.

Even greater irony falls on the list of businesses who view this as an 'exit strategy'. However, it could very well be one for a VC since their vision is through a lens different from yours if you have chosen to work towards being a legend. With absolutely no judgement.

Narayana Murthy, the founder of Infosys, aptly articulated that IPOs cannot be used as a surrogate for financing. The sole purpose of going public is to share the wealth with the people at large who may or may not have had the privilege or opportunity to indulge in creating or becoming a legend.[1]

MANTRA 11

THE GOLDEN ASSETS CLUB

People ... Only They Matter

"People will forget what you said, people will forget what you did, but people will never forget how you made them feel" –Maya Angelou

"In life, it is not so much what you do but what others do because of you" –Peter Burwash

On a recruitment mission for an extraordinarily successful private label brand where I had been the first employee, a question I was constantly asked related to why employees stuck with our company compared to larger, more well-known organisations.

During a session when I was providing politically correct reasons, I suddenly realised there was no real strategy, however much I claimed there was.

This MANTRA is about recognising and nurturing businesses' all-important golden assets—people.

It was 12.15 in the afternoon and a major presentation to the board that could last for a couple of hours was scheduled for 6.30 p.m.

Sandeep (name changed), our marketing manager, seemed a bit on edge and though typically very enthusiastic, his eyes betrayed a certain melancholy. It then suddenly struck me. It was his 3-year-old daughter Divya's birthday. God, how did I miss this? I called Sandeep aside and told him, "Sandeep, my sincere apologies for having fixed this meeting today. I completely forgot Divya's birthday. Please jump into your car and head home. I will manage the presentation this time. Not an issue at all!"

Sandeep could not believe what he had heard. It was like a miracle for which he had been praying. His eyes turned moistened as he thanked me profusely and left.

At that moment, I had touched his heart. From then on, he would not work for the money but for someone's heart.

My gesture was no orchestrated strategy. It was spontaneous and authentic, with genuine concern translating to empathy. That one gesture generated a ripple effect, creating more gratifying outcomes. For one, the others in the group knew right there that their personal dreams and aspirations would never be compromised at the altar of the organisation they worked for but, instead, would be amplified.

And Sandeep, on his drive home, would be pondering how he, in turn, could make a unique difference to his job and workplace now and in future.
That night Sandeep would be a changed man.
An episode I never fail to narrate when posed with the question of attrition.

I am constantly reminded of one of my bosses, an exceptionally successful managing director at one of the erstwhile Tata companies. His recruitment philosophy was simple. He recognised very early that while the degrees, experience and domain knowledge were undoubtedly crucial, one factor that would outsmart all that is the ability to wire ourselves differently.
If we could get people wired to a particular attitude (the Right Leg of the Golden Ladder), ordinary people would rise to achieve the impossible, prove themselves to be extraordinary and be truly unstoppable.
A vital element of that wiring is gratitude, which, as we will see, converts into loyalty.

In Sandeep's example, he felt gratitude after joining the company. What if there was a way to instil gratitude in employees even before they joined?
This MD would pick people who sought his help for employment, people who had to leave organisations and lacked a successful track record. Taking a chance on them he would provide them the opportunities to enhance their domain knowledge and skills. This onboarding would cement an attitude in the employee

to put the company's success above their own, treating their progress as a resultant derivative and not independent of it.

If you buy into someone's heart, you don't need to rely on their hands.

When someone ordinary is wired in this way, they will never fail and every failing attempt would only bring them an inch closer to the goal. They would undertake everything in their purview to ensure the mission they have been trusted with is accomplished.

Why and how does this happen? The MD knew one powerful secret.

That each one of us is a *powerhouse*, equipped with 50 trillion cells in our brains, with each cell possessing a voltage of 0.07 v. This makes each human being a 3.5 trillion voltage generator.[1] Unfortunately, most move about like a 40W bulb, oblivious to what can be unleashed. There are undoubtedly occasional streaks of brilliance, but too soon, they fade away into oblivion. But we become *unstoppable* if we are aware, recognise this strength and know the mechanism to convert it into action. People then transform themselves into the proverbial David who mastered 'powering' the Right Leg and race into the book of legends, vanquishing every Goliath.

The MD was fully cognizant of this power and leveraged that to the benefit of both the individual and the organisation.

Apart from energising people, actions such as these bond them to the organisation, making them never seek greener pastures because here is where they have found their true calling. Their purpose. Their potential.

And that is how people stay glued to that workplace with their hearts.

A dust storm was brewing strongly in the desert. The mercury was soaring at 47°C. It was Dubai. But inside the coolness of the air-conditioned room, it was different. There was a quiet anticipation. People from the Middle East and Europe regions had gathered for the much-awaited annual conference. An event that was to bring out the absolute best in everyone.

My presentation was about to begin. But the audio-visual gadget (during the Nineties, presentations were done in audio and video tracks separately) was not to be found. After much discussion, it came to light that the HR/Admin manager had forgotten to carry it from another location many miles away after the rehearsal session.
The tension in the air could be cut with a knife. And the HR manager was beaded in sweat. This was a defining moment. I had an option as the CEO: To vent my feelings and blame and embarrass him in front of the entire audience or did another option exist?

What flashed through my mind was that mistakes happen. Not all the time, but they do. Big ones, sometimes. But no one makes a mistake deliberately. This situation puts the person at fault in as much agony for failing as the other at the receiving end of this mistake. At that moment, anger and rebuke would only hurt a person's ego, causing more collateral damage than benefit.

If your child were to drop an expensive vase, you would not disown them in public. Yes, there would be moments of agitation, but they would pass. *That generates ownership.*

When you know you can take risks and fail, for which you would not be reprimanded, you will create miracles.

Sourav Ganguly, one of India's most successful cricket captains, was apparently known to tell his team members that for the next seven matches, they would not be dropped from the team, irrespective of their performance. This protocol immediately took the fear away from their minds and imparted stability by minimising insecurity, thus increasing ownership.

It is obvious what I told everyone at the conference that day. *"Mistakes do happen and I take complete ownership."* As you may have guessed, we delivered the presentation without the AV reel *and* successfully!

That day I had bought into the heart of the HR manager.

There lies the answer to how employees in our company never left its shores for another. There was only one word: Ownership. Coupled with empathy. To view each employee as a human with aspirations, emotions and vulnerabilities rather than just a name with a designation or a number.

Providing an opportunity to fail without any negative repercussions is the best form of generating ownership.

Foolish are those who delude themselves into believing they can achieve anything independently. No one has crossed any finish line merely because of their individual capacity.

There are always the few, sometimes silent, who contribute to your much-envied place at the top. Those who gave up their personal dreams to share the common vision with you, those who set aside their own priorities to make the time required for a specific project and those who sacrificed a multitude of opportunities that came their way to ensure your path was devoid of the dust and stones that would hamper your progress.

It is a given that no company can make any strides without people and that too the right ones, but the one key factor that would define the organisation's future course is the answer to the following question.

Do employees view the company as a means to an end that would only elevate them or do they perceive themselves as a cohesive unit where their upward mobility is closely linked to the organisation's aspirations?

So, isn't it crucial to get into their skin and understand what truly moves them and makes them push that extra mile without being told or supervised, but as if their life depended on what they do while providing immense joy to others and themselves? Declarations such as 'employees are our best asset' and 'we care for our employees more than we care for ourselves' sound wonderful, but are these words identifying with the dreams of the same employees? When one witnesses how top organisations today are engaging in 'getting rid' of thousands of employees at the drop of a hat, one wonders what happened to all the above statements and of being 'one family'. These then sound like empty words making the employees suspicious and never feeling a sense of 'ownership'. You will always be on a slippery slope if the employee is only aiming for personal advancement rather than being part of the organisation's success wheels.

Creating *ownership* is the only solution to this perennial issue, which could stop most companies from the bugbear of attrition.

It is a known fact that to hire, train or untrain a recruit and put them through the rigours of the job to ensure they deliver impressive results is a stupendous investment in terms of time, effort and financial resources. Every time an employee leaves, it creates both a visible and sometimes a largely invisible void. Ownership is the only solution that has a lasting effect.

Many are aware, but few have their fingers on this pulse. Your ability to ensure the employees believe in your vision is the sole key to keeping attrition at a minimum and propelling them to go beyond the ordinary. Thus, they access zones where miracles are performed through which they perceive their individual success. One word defines this entire space. Ownership.

Yet another power-packed method of generating ownership is seen in this quote from Nike's Phil Knight.

"Don't tell people how to do things; tell them what to do and let them surprise you with their results."

3M, an organisation known for significant innovations, lets employees use 15 per cent of their time to pursue inventive ideas that excited them.[2] These would have the organisation's full sanction in terms of credit for the outcome and whatever other rewards it came with. More importantly, the employees had complete freedom to fail.

The company discovered that this act brought to the fore the unique strengths of the employee resulting in remarkable achievements.

Spencer Silver and Art Fry, two of the scientists at 3M, who were given this independence, accidentally discovered what today is the revolutionary Post-it Note.[3] They were hailed as the heroes of their time and given the entire credit for bringing this wonderful, self-generated innovation to the world, which accounts for a significant percentage of 3M's revenues and profits.

Yet another time when an employee assumes complete ownership is when there is a feeling of having 'created' something that has their signature on it. The pride of seeing their creation turning into reality and their accomplishments appreciated by everyone is a joy in itself.

Google, too, adopts this policy very effectively. Employees are provided with twenty per cent time, which translates to one day in a week, where they are given the luxury to dabble in ideas and products that would have their names on them. Therefore, it is not surprising that some of Google's most fabulous creations, Gmail and Google Maps, are the result of such an endeavour. These products and services generate not only an appreciable proportion of Google's revenue, close to 50 per cent, but also add priceless visibility and brand enhancement to the employee. Imagine an individual's delight when they know that their contribution has played a pivotal role in moving the wheels of one of the most outstanding companies of all time.

Do This ACTION Exercise Now!

Identify a minimum of three avenues to win over three employees and seal the bond of ownership with them.

Experiment with at least one employee in the next thirty days.

MANTRA 12

ARE YOU HEARING A NO WHENEVER YOU SAY YES?

How You Can Be the Smartest Negotiator in Any Room

> *"Never negotiate out of fear. But never fear to negotiate."-John. F. Kennedy*

The breath of life holds sustenance only when through negotiation, all beings come in unison.

In this complex world, most believe it is a 'dog eat dog' situation and trampling on another is the modus operandi to rise up the corporate or any personal ladder. While this is untrue, there is a mysterious power that few recognise and is often the key that opens the crucial doors.

We do this every day and with everyone.
NEGOTIATE.

Trying to get our story in. Convince the other of our opinion. Be it a client. A prospective buyer. Our spouses. Or even our children. Many times, they move away angry, bitter or unhappy leaving everyone equally troubled..

It does not have to be that way.

How often haven't I been called to a negotiation table with the words, "Vijay, let's make it a win-win." But within a few minutes, it becomes clear that the conciliatory tone is merely a ruse to get one's way.

Once you understand this robust science of how you can gain by benefiting others in areas *they do not outwardly express*, you have mastered the art.

You need to, maybe, negotiate the purchase of a real estate premise, a dealership contract, a deal with your union, investment options with a VC or a large purchase deal, all of which could run into millions of dollars and dip into years of future earnings. Not being equipped with this skill can be a potential disaster.

This MANTRA opens doors into that world where the solution to successful business relationships is unmasked.

In their book, *Getting to YES*, Roger Fisher and William Ury introduce the powerful concept of Principled Negotiation[1]. Often, we enter a negotiation with a specific objective to be achieved and if that is not fruitful, we believe we have failed. Herein lies the biggest fallacy, where large fissures occur in self-worth and relationships apart from the business itself.

How often, even at home, we desire something significant but give way as the relationship takes priority.

This 'compromise' sours that very relationship since the one who walks away thinking they have 'compromised' often feels ill done by, not having been able to get what they want. It then festers in their mind as to how extremely unfair it is that they must give in all the time (even if that weren't the case), pushing the person into victim mode and leaving a simmering resentment.

Two great learnings from this book that can create a win-win are:

1. *To separate ourselves from what we want in a situation.*

For instance, not achieving a particular outcome should have nothing to do with how you view yourself. Thus, at no point should a lack of accomplishment in any project or objective be allowed to be a reflection of what or who we are.

This distinction is critical as it separates us from the issue and helps the opposite party at the negotiating table in a similar manner. This one act alone cuts stress levels by at least fifty per cent leaving enough mind space to think better.

2. *To focus on the underlying interests and not on positions.*

We often see ourselves and others getting 'stuck' to a position. This rigid attachment to the position is where the ego comes in and not discerning the true reason behind is the cause of all the multiple failed negotiations. Recognise that this positional attachment arises from a deep but hidden interest. Seek to unearth that 'position' from the chasms of the mind.

It was a hot afternoon when I received a call from one of my community members where I, as the prime mover, had worked hard to revive a swimming pool that had fallen into disuse for many years.

After a gruelling 60 days, we had a shimmering pool rippling in the afternoon sun. The caller was vehement about how a particular pump was unnecessary, how we had wasted money in what was done and how specific processes were overlooked.

This offensive took me by surprise. For one, this was not his area of responsibility. Then, I had not seen him get involved in this even minimally. That was totally acceptable. But having resolved numerous complex issues on this project and made a success of it, I felt it was a personal attack.

I immediately launched into a tirade about how right I was and how I should not be questioned. This infuriated the other person, who was now generating more reasons why I was wrong. All this was heading nowhere. This argument was turning into a full-blown battle, threatening years of our relationship, with both of us unwilling to give in.

That is when the second-most essential element of the book by Fisher and Ury sprung to my memory.

'Never stick to your position. Go behind and look for deeper needs and interests and fears.'

I stopped arguing. I just listened and tried to see what lay behind this unusual behaviour of spending time and effort bashing my work. There had to be something larger than this superficial reason. It just did not make sense.

So, we put off our discussion for another day and met in a more conducive ambience, with me fully convinced that there had to be some other profound reason for his outward aggression.

As we conversed and I kept listing all the beauty additions near the pool, he muttered silently, "But it's not so beautiful from my place."

I was taken aback. It all suddenly made sense to me.

What he was challenging was not my work or competence. He was reluctant to admit his inability to have an unobstructed view of the pool because of a pump blocking it.

He was taking a 'position', but the reason behind that was a 'desire'. The desire for a beautiful view from the balcony was being denied. It was inconsequential to him that nobody else in the condominium had expressed displeasure.

But it mattered to him. I would have never gotten to that if I were not looking for something underneath and continued the argument.

So, all that was required was satisfying a simple wish to have that pump moved from that place. Period. A wish which was never overtly expressed but cloaked in technical jargon about its viability and necessity.

Peace was restored when this need was identified and fulfilled by shifting the pump to another location.

As radical as it may sound, this scenario plays out in multiple avenues of our lives. Constantly. Sometimes when entrepreneurs and business owners approach VCs for funding. It is crucial to understand why an investor is exhibiting a particular behaviour rather than be swayed by their external mannerisms. This reflection is the key to establishing credence and conviction about one's project and gaining investors' confidence.

Being provoked to anger and displaying a sense of disappointment tends to make the entrepreneur 'rigid' in their stance. This rigidity invariably makes them let go of an opportunity due to their adhering to a 'position.'

How often have we not seen an entrepreneur lose a potential investment because they refused to budge from a stance - based purely on the perceived behavioural patterns of others rather than delving into the underlying reasons behind them?

SUMMARY

Ask yourself in every negotiation:

Are you taking a position for the sake of it? Is the individual or group in the opposition unit succumbing to that same attitude? Or can you identify for yourself and others if there are deep, underlying, unspoken desires or fears? If you do, address them.

Do This ACTION Exercise Now!

Recreate a previous situation where you had felt miserable about a negotiation that had gone haywire or examine any current situation that requires a friend, client or vendor to come to the negotiation table. See how you can apply the above two principles and generate the master plan for a true win-win situation.

PART TWO

MANTRAS TO POWER THE SECOND (RIGHT) LEG

MANTRA 13

INSIDE THE VAULT OF RICHES

Re-Programming the Mind for Unstoppable Success

> “
>
> *You may or may not have control over what happens to you. But you have one hundred per cent control over what **you do** with what happens to you.*

September 29, 1982. In the city of Chicago, three people die after consuming a pill for headaches. By October 1, that number rises to seven.

The pill: Tylenol, Johnson & Johnson's most significant earner. Within weeks, the market share of that business crashes from a high of 37 per cent to a dismal low of 7 per cent.

James (Jim) Burke, the CEO, had to act. And fast. He then takes a decision that no one, for decades prior, had embarked upon. That of ordering the recall of thirty-one million bottles of Tylenol from across the country overnight.

A call that would see millions of the company's dollars go up in smoke. Not to mention putting his own exceptionally successful career at stake.

But he does just that. Across the United States, Tylenol is sucked away from the shelves at a dizzying speed back to J&J's labs.

As the media tears into the company and the lunatic who infused cyanide into the Tylenol pills continues to be at large, Burke stands firm. And his entire team goes into high action mode, ensuring Johnson & Johnson, is back in the market within three weeks with Tylenol in a new three-way tamper-proof packaging,

Burke also embarks upon a $100-million advertising blitz, one of history's largest, to communicate the company's actions to the entire nation. Of continuing to build a safer world and accompanied by an unconditional apology. The act demonstrates J&J's commitment to the most important person on this planet: its customer.

These actions of Jim Burke did not spring from his education, experience or technology background. In fact, at times they were a hindrance as they loudly declared why he should not be doing what he was.

The outcome: The business bounced back, resulting in the company's market share climbing again and touching the 30 per cent mark by 1983, in just over a year. It was an action plan and a resurgence unprecedented and unheard of even today![1]

The response of Burke was extraordinary. It was as if it came from an undiscovered place. A space yet uncharted in all we have covered in the chapters of the Left Leg of the Golden Ladder, the domain expertise. Where words like *courage* now begin to find a place in the dictionary. Words which seem to find their way quickly into the hearts of a select few but seem to be eluding millions. Not possessing these or displaying actions contrary to these could have fatal consequences. But embracing and internalising them puts one on the path to becoming a legend.

This journey marks the beginning of powering the 'Right Leg' of the Golden Ladder.

Which would be the other *'necessary and special condition'* for someone to rise to the top of the Golden Ladder.

This MANTRA is about that necessary and special condition, without which no one can rise above a particular level, which is the key to taking their place among the legends.

Now for a recap of what The Golden Ladder stands for.

While imbibing the giants' sacred and almost secretive business principles is the first powerful weapon (the Left Leg), it is incomplete without the Right Leg of the Golden Ladder firmly positioned, anchored and energised for the journey towards legacy to begin.

To recap, Golden Ladder is that magical stairway that alone can transport individuals from the zone of 'good' to the realm of the 'exemplary', the land of the fabled who take their place in history, those whose legacy inspires people to go beyond themselves.

And the key which eludes most is the reality that unless both the legs are powered and anchored perfectly, this ladder has the potential to slip, bringing even the greatest of geniuses down.
What we have discussed up to now is the powering of the Left Leg, the leg of domain dominance.

We now begin our journey to power the ***'Right Leg'.***

The first set of mantras (Part One) dwelt on the ability to attain *domain mastery* to achieve a formidable business using unique techniques the business legends successfully figured out. But those techniques in isolation do not guarantee either the continued success or the longevity of any venture.
The one element that ensures longevity is what is covered herein and forms the scope of the following chapters—***The Right Leg.***
This Right Leg has the immense power to topple the ladder quickly if not structured and energised perfectly. Fuelled and fired immaculately, it can even compensate for the deficiencies of the Left Leg and lead one to the top.
That is its remarkable strength. And its supremacy.

Mapping The Right Leg's terrain

This leg is undoubtedly the 'soul' of the ladder. This leg is the *world's most potent instrument.* **THE MIND.**
We all possess this, but we have been denied the instruction manual. It is up to each of us to script it for the journey of our life.
The only limitation of such a process of having to discover and create this *'manual'* by ourselves is that many lessons which

could be learned from the follies of others need to be re-learnt, thus eroding precious time and bandwidth.

But it does not have to be that way.

Everyone does not have to reinvent the wheel every time to be able to drive the most fantastic car in the world.

In the limited time on this planet, if there were a method to obtain the crux from the legends who have ruled the world in this sphere, it would make our journey much more successful and help accelerate our progress towards attaining their status.

This mantra is that essence in concentrated form. Taken from the masters who have pioneered creating the world's best instruction manual.

To power the **Right Leg, the mind.**

Knowing, understanding, living and working by these principles will ensure the mastery of the ***Right Leg***, which then sets the stage for the ascent to the top of the Golden Ladder.

The real road to the fabled legendary kingdom begins now!

Let us shift our attention to that lazy afternoon when even the streets of Bangalore take a breather from the torments of the million tonnes of steel that trample them each day. I was meeting Arun, a friend, at a quaint coffee shop, to advise him on how to invigorate his sluggish furniture business. It had been running for ten years but was going nowhere special.

I started by asking the fundamental question of the exact problem he faced.

He launched into a tirade about how i) the competition was severe, especially after Covid, ii) employees lacked loyalty and switched jobs at the first available opportunity and iii) funds, vital for business growth, were scarce.

I let him finish and said, "Arun, that is great. You could articulate everything so well. I have a simple question for you. Assume you have all the funds in the world. Assume you have the best talent and they will not leave.

"Further, assume the business environment is excellent and whatever products you position in the marketplace will sell.

"In this scenario, with all your concerns taken care, from your current revenue of Rs.1 crore per year, what levels would you reach/achieve in five years?"

Pause for a few minutes.

Write down in your worksheet what you think Arun predicted his revenue would be at the end of five years from his current Rs.1 crore level with all his hurdles removed.

Do not turn the page till you have written the number.

Arun said, "Rs.10 crores."

I asked him, "Why not Rs.100 crores?"

He nearly fell off his seat. He said, "I cannot even think of Rs.25 crores, let alone Rs.100 crores."

That marks the first step in imbibing the lessons of the instruction manual for the Right Leg.

To decide what it takes to be that incredible diamond.

There was no pressure on Arun to forecast only Rs. 10 crores, so, what made him limit himself to that figure?

This ceiling that he created was within himself.

This is a critical insight that should be confronted in the initial steps of this new journey.

During my days in the telecom industry, I had the opportunity to visit the famous Dhirubhai Ambani Knowledge Centre (DAKC) in Mumbai.

A place of enormous proportions. There could have been many others matching this grandeur, but there was one startling difference.

In the centre of the enormous courtyard was an incredibly huge sign, approximately two hundred feet in width and twenty feet in height. It had just one sentence printed on it, to the effect that *one is defined only by the limits one set for themselves.* It is no wonder that you see Mukesh Ambani growing from strength to strength and surprising everyone, making it evident that he has followed this quote to the letter and sets only the stars as his limit, if he sets one at all.

How accurate that quote is!

We seem to be scared to think big. We seem to lack the courage. We seem to believe that failure lies not in setting low goals but in setting ambitious goals and falling short to achieve them. Not recognising that our success lies only in setting lofty goals and gearing ourselves up to meet them.
Remember the famous line:
"Shoot for the moon. Even if you miss, you'll land among the stars."
Do not set limits that are small and diminutive.
Generate the courage to set limits that are worthy of giants.

So, when the next opportunity presents itself in the form of setting a goal for either your project or a significant task you need to accomplish, you have two choices.
Either listen to the voice of fear that pulls you down or break every ceiling your mind puts up and train your sights so high it makes the Gods proud.

Remember, it is YOU who is setting those limits. No one is stopping you or controlling you except you.
Stop and listen to the inner dialogue, the dominant thought, on any day. To the sounds. Not of the external world, but to that incessant chatter inside your head. Listen to the conversation that is constantly happening between the *two yous.*
"Why did this happen?" "Why has that not happened?" "Why is someone behaving or not behaving in a particular way?" And it continues—a turbulent, unending stream that shows no sign of letting up.

If you cut the noise and reflect, you will discover a common thread that runs through this entire conversation in your head. Throughout the day. It will point to either abundance or lack. Whichever direction it is biased towards will be the DOMINANT THOUGHT of your life.

Like a looped record that seems to have a life of its own. Here is the breaking news.

WE BECOME WHAT OUR DOMINANT THOUGHT IS.

If our constant chatter demonstrates a lack, then our outside world will throw lack at us and reflect scarcity in our lives. In every aspect. If our dominant thought is fear, then 'pulling back' will become the norm.

On the other hand, if our constant chatter is one of abundance, then our outside world will mirror abundance and reflect that in every aspect of our lives. Similarly, if our chatter revolves around courage, then leaping forward at every opportunity would define our actions.

This recognition is the first step to mind mastery.

Knowing that, if your dominant thought is of anger or revenge, you then become that unfriendly and irritated person, wondering why your relationships suck.

If your dominant thought is of feeling blessed for all you have, either in business or health, abundance will seek you in wealth and health. In terms of affluence and plenitude.

But if your dominant thought revolves around a challenging business environment or a difficult life in general, which focuses on lack, then those conditions of paucity and deficiency will prevail. Business stagnancy, if not losses, poor health and hurdles in every step will be the order of the day.

Recognising this, how do you harness your mind to power your life?

Is there a proven method that can identify our dominant thought and enable us to move the needle towards progress, prosperity and success?

The answer is Yes!

A simple yet powerful technique, ratified by none other than one of the top business schools in the world, provides the infallible solution to recognise and channelise our dominant thought, utilising what seems to be an inseparable part of us today—our smartphone.

While this device is vilified for taking over our lives, it can be deployed as a knife to cut through the strings of bondage.

Here is how. It takes just three uncomplicated but ingenious steps.

Set the alarm on the device to ring every two hours. At each ring, perform this powerful ritual.

Step 1:

Amid the chatter racing through your mind, bring to your awareness (be 'AWARE') the exact dominant thought that is running through your mind at that moment.

Is it anger at someone you feel has done some wrong or anxiety and apprehension regarding the outcome of a vital customer deal or a feeling of excitement that you are on the verge of a significant breakthrough in your product or service?

You can see clearly that some thoughts *elevate* you. Some *debilitate* you. A few *energise* you. A few others *discharge* your mental battery and enervate you.

And some empower you.

Step 2:

With this recognition of the outcome of each thought, STOP the mind's flow towards those thoughts if they do not energise, empower or elevate you. You have that power. This thought blocking creates a barrier to the incessant and unchecked flow of thoughts.

This has also now generated a space between the unceasing flow of thoughts that only serve to weaken you.

It is now critical to fill this space before it gets re-occupied with those negative thoughts.

At this moment, take a pause and follow this.

Think of a rose. With all its glorious red petals and its divine fragrance. Move from petal to petal. See how well-crafted the petals are. Observe the thorns that accompany them and think how painful they can be if you accidentally touch them.

Now shift your mind to focus on an elephant. Its large trunk. Its magnificence in size and stature. Its deep grey. Its tail, so diminutive in relation to its overall size. Its tusks which gleam in the daylight sun.

Now slowly, if you have been to a beach, recollect the ocean's enormity. The foamy waves that constantly make it to the shore only to be sent back to make yet another attempt.

The sand below your feet, stretching for miles, the distant fisherman looking for the next school of fish and the setting sun that seems to gain in glory as it descends.

Do you recognise how you could channel the mind along the thoughts you decide to direct it on? And guide it along the course of your choice? With this realisation, you have unearthed something powerful. You can *choose* to direct your mind to any thought you wish. Whenever you wish. That is such a liberating feeling. To possess that power. Recognise it and seize it.

On the contrary, if unnoticed, your mind would have followed a journey of its own. No surprise there. It is performing a job it knows best: Movement. From thought to thought. Constantly. Most of the time, it thrives on negativity. Not knowing this, we get spun into its web and flail along the thought highway, turning ourselves into powerless, enslaved persons.

We remain oblivious to this great power that has been bestowed upon us. The power to choose which thought to focus our mind on, a rose, an elephant, the beach or any kind of positivity.

Seize that power.

The power to keep your mind on whichever thought you want to, irrespective of where the mind wants to go.

Spelt above is the greatest lesson; if you can internalise this, it is sheer deliverance and opens the path for making headway from the zone of the ordinary to the realm of the revolutionary.

We now enter the most life-changing step.

Step 3:

Having stopped the flood of thoughts and generated the space in Step 2, you now need to '*create a thought*' to fill that space (recall how you could *create* the thought of the rose, the beach or the elephant). Access that amazing power you have to create any thought of your choice.

So, create a thought that empowers you. A thought that has the power to elevate you and energise you.

It could be how you would win the next tender, how your product has made waves in the market or how you generated a new idea that could transform an entire industry. How you could be hailed as the greatest unicorn in recent times. Or how you and your partner have the time of your lives in the world's most exotic spot.

Ironically, unaware of this power, many succumb to the negativity the mind leads them to.

Remember, the thought you create does not have to be true at this moment. Like any debilitating thought you could have been creating earlier (which, too, was never true), you can create this thought of high positive energy.

And now, SHIFT your mind to that thought that can elevate you to a state of accomplishment and glory.

In summary,

- **'A'** for being '**Aware**' of the thought your mind is currently on
- **'S'** for '**Stopping**' the mind if it were not focussed on a thought that elevates, empowers or energises you and
- **'S'** for '**Shifting**' your mind to a thought, you have the power to create, which empowers and energises you.

This is A.S.S. A potent medicinal formula and the beginning of the transformational journey to take you into the league of giants.

This pattern thus releases the 'ASS' in us and renders the power to be unassailable and *Unstoppable.*
Start with your business model. Using this powerful technique. Today.

Let's revert to Jim Burke.
The operative word that defined his actions at that moment of crisis was 'courage'. Courage that defied every obstacle, thus ensuring the dominant position of Johnson & Johnson. Courage to believe in himself and the courage to be committed to the company's Credo **(J&J Values, Mantra 2),** which put the customer's welfare above everything else. This courage allows a select few to step into the halls of the iconic. Setting the standards to ensure courage flows through every nerve of the organisation for generations. This courage is what distinguishes them from many an intelligent and exceptionally experienced entrepreneur who has the Left Leg firmly in place but is destabilised by fear, sometimes failing even at the mundane.
The select few instantly recognise that *courage is not the absence of fear but pushing through the act despite fear. Organisations that have designed their Vision Statement with a fabric of this quality are the long-distance winners.*

P&G, which has reigned for 175 years, has specific processes instilled to ensure courage is not the preserve of a select few but a quality that everyone has deep reserves of. In the words of its former Chairman & CEO, David Taylor, its most important secret is to train people to develop the 'courage to be uncomfortable'.[2] Individuals are dumped into the sea of uncertainty early in their careers, ensuring only those who surface live on. At P&G, I remember being thrown into the alligator swamp of selling products travelling to over 50 towns deep inside the country every month for nine months, wondering, in one of my bullock cart rides, if this was the reward for my MBA from IIMA. As Marc Pritchard, the CMO of P&G, had said, they work towards building the courage to say 'Yes' to revolutionary ideas such as the 'Thank you, Mom' campaign emphasising on the touching love of a mother for her child with the message, *"It takes someone strong. To make someone strong*". With the mother sometimes a transgender person.[3] The courage to be different, courage to go beyond every boundary.

Courage is a part of the inbuilt ecosystem at **Colgate-Palmolive**, where every leader is tested in the fires of uncertainty and failure. As recently as April 2021, the Director of Integrated Communications, Laurent Cayet, emphasised courage as the most critical driver, far more contagious than fear.[4] It also ran the famous 'Smile Above the Odds' campaign featuring various situations in which people were seen overcoming multiple life's challenges with a smile. Each documentary in the series concluding with the message 'Smile is our strength'.

For centuries, the company has held on to the power of the smile, the simplest form of communication and constantly nurtured stories of courage on every platform. This broadcast includes its latest message about how it is not just about smiling through adversity alone. It's about possessing the courage to *take action – no matter the challenge. Celebrating those who 'smile above all the odds'.*

Tesla is yet another company in today's world that is extremely courageous. It comes as no surprise as one turns through their manuscript's pages on values.
Tesla's core values include doing its best, *taking risks* and continuous learning.[5]

I believe that apart from the desire to be legendary, sheer courage prompted Elon Musk to acquire Twitter.
As is evident from all these great legends, the first operative word in powering the Right Leg is *courage,* something that goes beyond every definition of the domain of the Left Leg.
How, then, do we develop this extraordinary quality?
Courage underlies one vital ingredient, often unrecognised. It treads in the footsteps of the *faith* that helps magnify one's actions exponentially.
Faith does not set its foundation in just what you can achieve *but in your ability to face every situation and manoeuvre and emerge successfully.*

As mentioned in an earlier chapter on emotion (Mantra 4), the two most potent driving forces are 'fear' and 'desire'. Desire propels us. Fear hampers us. Unfortunately, millions are the great minds that have lost their way in the pit of *fear.*
All this has its origin in one specific foundation. That of BELIEF.
Perpetuating belief creates faith. Let's explore that mystic zone.

BELIEF: THE NOURISHMENT OF LIFE'S SCREEN

On a hot afternoon, a seventeen-year-old wandered listlessly in the streets of Kolkata. It was evident something was weighing heavily on him. He suddenly spotted an older man with a long, white beard by the pavement who was preparing to set up his makeshift workstation. Something about that man made this boy stop and take a second look. Curious, he approached the man and asked him what he was doing.

The old man replied, "Son, I foretell the future."

This boy was fascinated. Though he knew of fortune-tellers, this was the first time he was able to talk to one. "Really? How do you do that?" he asked. There was something about this man that seemed divine to the boy.

The older man went about expounding how this science, known as astrology, was based on powerful insights gleaned from a study of planetary movements and their influence on all living and non-living beings.

He described how the mighty sea was just a puppet under the influence of this celestial body, the moon, how the moon's waxing and waning had an enormous influence on the movement of the tides. He went on to add that if such a massive expanse of water could be subject to an enormous magnetic effect and when almost 80 per cent of the human body is made up of water, definitely the various combinations of planetary forces play a vital role in our journey of life!

The boy was dazzled. He then asked the obvious question: "Sir, could you please foretell my future? I am lost with nothing significant or exciting happening in my life and don't see a light at the end of the tunnel."

The man agreed and sought a few details, with which the boy readily parted.

After shuffling what seemed like a complex set of numbers, referring to a tatty manual and fiddling with numerous other 'sacred texts' with fervent concentration, the old man got up abruptly and exclaimed, "I don't believe this!"

The boy was taken aback and fearfully asked, "What happened, Sir?"

The man said, "Young man, what you are about to hear is a miracle. A one in a million chance of its occurrence and one of a momentous nature."

The boy was unsure of what the man was about to deliver. Then the older man revealed his finding, his eyes shining beyond the normal. He said, "Son, do you know that you are the reincarnation of none other than the great Napoleon Bonaparte?

"The one whose prowess and achievement could be matched by none. You will soon be shining along the length and breadth of this nation with the brilliance of a million suns." The boy was stunned. In a complete daze, he asked the old man, "Are you absolutely sure?"

The man said, "As sure as you are standing before me! I have examined and thought through all the observations in complete detail and have no doubt whatsoever.

"Son, you are on the verge of conquering the world of today. Go ahead and vanquish every obstacle and forge ahead. The Universe awaits you."

The boy stood transfixed. Rousing himself, he thanked the older man, paid him more than was asked and was on his way. Now suddenly, there was a spring in his step. He was not the same boy who met the astrologer a little while ago in despair. This was someone new. Someone who tore through the curtain of uncertainty. He could now see himself as a top achiever and a key mover in everything he did. He had metamorphosised. The caterpillar was on the verge of transforming into a wonderful butterfly.

He then went on to become one of the greatest masterminds of that era. Excelling in every area of business and science. And creating some admirable engineering marvels that the world watched in wonder. But wait, there's more. A few days after the prediction, the astrologer realised he had made a mistake and tried to contact him. But it was too late. So much the better, since the new 'Napoleon' was well on his way!

Around the same time, a siren rang in one of the small factories in the scenic region of Baden, West Germany. It was five in the evening, the time the factory closed for the weekend. The buzz of good cheer and anticipation on happy faces filled the air as each was excited about what they had planned. John (name changed) was one such. He had promised his son the long-awaited drive through the countryside, stopping by wayside cafes, sipping coffee and bonding with the child.

As he stepped out, he suddenly remembered leaving his wallet on the table inside the freezer room. He rushed back to retrieve it and when he entered, he saw the light was on at the far end of the room. As he went to turn it off, he heard a loud noise. He turned to see that the freezer room door had shut behind him. John's heart sank. He could get locked in as he had not turned off the alarm. As he reached the door and tugged, it would not budge. It had gotten locked from the outside. With a sinking feeling, he realised no amount of yanking and pulling at the bulky handle would make any difference. He frightfully knew he was locked in. John frantically started shouting for help, but everyone had left. His voice barely escaped that enormous door. He was in a state of panic. His thoughts were racing as he pictured himself freezing to death in the minus-twenty-degree temperature of the room. Even in that freezing atmosphere, he was sweating profusely. His heart was pounding as if on a treadmill.

Over the next thirty minutes, his voice gradually faded to a whisper as hopelessness took over. He started feeling dizzy. A little later, he made a few more feeble attempts at the door and, in less than an hour, felt his head spinning. He fainted.

The morning sun rose to welcome the workers to the factory on Monday. One of them opened the freezer room and was shocked to find his colleague in the middle of the floor. He rushed to check his pulse. There was none. John had died.

But here is the astonishing and strange twist to this tale. At 5.05 p.m. that evening, precisely two minutes after John entered the freezer room, the electricity had failed due to a fault in the circuit. In effect, there was no power in the freezer room after 5.05 p.m. to make the room any colder. Ironically, when the door was opened that Monday morning, the temperature in the room was 17°C, way above the -20°C it was supposed to be. And there was no dearth of water or food in that zone.

John did not die that night due to the cold. Nor was it hunger or thirst that killed him. He died because of something else.

He died because he ***believed*** and was convinced he would freeze to death that night. And he brought that to fruition.

While that young boy in Kolkata ***believed*** he was the reincarnation of Napoleon Bonaparte, with success as his second nature – and he brought that to fruition too.

This MANTRA to power the Right Leg of the Golden Ladder boils down to a pivotal factor.

What you intensely believe, you will achieve.

Yes, whatever you believe intensely is what you will achieve. Nothing more. Nothing less.

The fascinating news is that what you believe does not have to be *true*. Or right. You can believe *anything* and that will materialise in your life.

If you believe you can achieve a business turnover of only Rs.10 crores, that will be the highest you will achieve. If you believe you will be the greatest legend reigning for the next hundred years and beyond, you will be. If you believe you are bad at math, you will be. If you believe you can accomplish anything, accomplishment will shadow you all the time. *Belief is everything.*

So, here is the million-dollar question.

If the path to legendary success was that simple, why are only so few so successful?

The answer lies in the related question,

How do you 'believe'?

When you struggle with cash flow, have employees deserting you and have sales declining, how do you believe you could hit the Rs.1,000 crore revenue mark over the next ten years from a current Rs.10 crore figure?

If someone is grappling with a mid-level job in their forties, how do they believe that they could become the CEO of that company in the coming five years?

Is it at all possible?

And here is the trillion-dollar answer.

Yes, yes, yes! It is most definitely possible! You can move mountains if you *believe.*

"*If you believe you can, you can. And if you believe you cannot, you cannot.*" Whatever we believe, however preposterous, we will achieve.

So, how do you 'believe'?

To answer this, we must take a detour and delve into the mystery and modalities of this powerful instrument, the mind.

The CONSCIOUS Mind vs The SUBCONSCIOUS Mind

Our mind is composed of two constituents: The *conscious* and the *subconscious.*

Like the iceberg that floats on water with only ten per cent visible above while ninety per cent lies submerged, the conscious mind, too, is only a tenth of this incredible instrument. The one that is capable of analysis, planning and short-term memory. What we use to communicate externally on a superficial basis. The remaining ninety per cent is the subconscious that effectively drives our lives. Yes, every single activity, including all the involuntary responses and autonomous body systems, but hidden and unavailable for easy access. While the conscious and subconscious are separated only by a wafer-thin partition it is exceptionally difficult to gain entry into the subconscious.

Here is the game-changing news!
Whatever you *program into your subconscious* is what you will believe, thereby making you achieve that very exact thing.
Whatever you are witnessing on the channel of your life, your current state of business, your current state of wealth, your current state of health and relationships is what you have fed into your subconscious, knowingly or unknowingly and have therefore *believed.* And have thus watched it unfold.

Assume you are watching a program on TV. You do not like what you are watching. That does not make you buy another TV, change it or go to another location to watch the program of your liking. That would not be very smart.
So, what do you do?
You change the channel.

Likewise, if you wish to change what you are viewing on the screen of your life, you need to change the channel. Which would then change the feed into the subconscious and, thereby, your beliefs. And consequently, your perceived reality.
Lack of this understanding is the leading cause for all your hard work and intelligence not necessarily yielding the required results. Your beliefs. They decide your destiny.

So, what, then, is the channel of our lives?

It is the frequency of our thought. Reflect on this.

Assume that someone rushes in and says a speeding motorist has hit your car. Your immediate reaction is one of anger, frustration and sadness. Seconds later, though, someone tells you that the vehicle was not yours. Your new feeling is one of happiness, joy and relief. Whatever happened to you just then, the happiness or sadness in those limited moments, was based solely on the frequency your thought was tuned to. Nothing else.

Each thought carries with it a particular frequency and magnetic field.

When frequencies resonate, they produce magic and when they conflict, they generate chaos.

On a quiet early morning, when you are thinking intensely about someone, you receive a call from the same person! Your thought frequencies matched. They harmonised. Magic is produced.

I remember an episode when, one stormy night, my mother was deeply concerned about not having received any news from me for several days. I was in a faraway city (Kanpur) at that time with no immediate mode of communication. Those were the days when a letter would take up to seven days to reach the recipient. In deep disquietude, she sat down to write yet another letter.

The next day, the doorbell rang and to her complete disbelief, my mother saw me standing in front of her. The intensity of her desire to see me, which set her frequency to match mine, had made me take the immediate train for Chennai, my hometown, without any ostensible reason, despite a busy work schedule. My father, who was a strong proponent of 'belief' and its working principles, knew what exactly had transpired as he smiled to himself.

Each of us generates forty to fifty thousand thoughts every day. A good three-fourths of them are repetitive, while close to ninety per cent of them are negative. Cloaked in 'all that should not happen' and 'what-ifs' about the worst possible happenings. Effectively in today's age and times, our minds constantly emit frequencies of fear, doubt and uncertainty. It is, therefore, not a great wonder to see that anxiety, depression and worry are our constant companions.

So, what is the solution if we were to achieve the highest that we desire? The best in every avenue of our business and daily lives. What changes our self-limiting beliefs?

You do this by reprogramming your subconscious.

And here is how, using the blueprint handed down by the masters over the centuries.

RE-PROGRAMMING THE SUBCONSCIOUS

In the temporary suspension of mental activity, you must recognise that *thoughts are unreal.* They are created by *us*. And only us. With no tangible reality. They are ephemeral. And most importantly, have nothing to do with what is happening *now.*

Stop and wait for what the next thought could be. You could wait forever. You will not see one. Because thought has life only

in the past or in the future. Never in the 'now'. That is a great discovery. That liberates us. If we choose to.
Often, the future is suspended in thoughts of worry while the past is energised with regret or nostalgia. All these hamper the speed with which we desire to proceed towards our destination.

To reprogram the subconscious and feed it with thoughts that would morph into powerful beliefs requires unravelling its programming code. It is almost impossible to penetrate the small, delicate divide between the conscious and the subconscious, without this crucial knowledge. But at the same time, there are time-tested, powerful neurological techniques that can influence and create new neural pathways in the brain, activating the switch that opens this door to the subconscious.

Here then, is a robust *five-step process* that has the ammunition to penetrate the subconscious and feed it any thought, converting it into a compelling and unshakeable belief. A belief that will transmute any desire into reality.

STEP 1: The Power of the Two Magical Words

There are two magical words that, when uttered in unison, have the potency to bring to life all that comes after them.
They are 'I' and 'AM.' When expressed together, they are dynamite. They have the potential to bring down a mountain or to make the seas evaporate.

When someone says, '**I AM** stressed', be sure that stress will follow them like a shadow.
Similarly, saying '**I AM** poor' will lead one down the poverty lane.

In the same breath, an affirmation of '**I AM** strong' assumes the strength of a thousand giants to bring unassailable vitality and vigour into your life.
Likewise, the sentence '**I AM** prosperous' has the weaponry to bring to the fore every possibility of unlimited affluence and abundance in multiple avenues in life.

Now, pause and reflect on what you are constantly telling yourself. The words *after 'I AM'*.
Are they words of abundance or are they words of uncertainty and doubt? Are they words of achievement or those of fear and worry? Are they words of unbounded plentifulness in everything you see around you or words of lack?
Do you hear yourself constantly say, "I AM hassled", but wonder why there is so much tension and trepidation all around?
Whatever you utter after the words "I AM", the subconscious echoes, "Your word is my command" and bingo, the situation lands in front of you!

Are these sentences familiar?
"I AM no good at the stock market."
"I AM perennially short of money."
Do you then wonder why everyone except you is a stock market genius? And why you constantly seem to have more days than money in a month?
A constant utterance of "I AM afraid" is not a recipe for achieving the tag of the most courageous person.
In areas of your life where life is a dream, maybe, music, poetry, conversation or any skill, lean back and ponder at the words you

choose after I AM. They will most likely be "I AM extremely proficient at music" or "I AM great at conversations". And that's being projected back to you as images of your life.

This is the **first magical key** to unlocking the subconscious. By feeding it with what you desire using specific techniques. Beginning with the 'I AM' strategy.

And thereupon translate that into a *belief*.

Eventually, you will witness what you desire on the screen of your life.

Do This ACTION Exercise NOW!

1. Write down your top three desires.
2. Create sentences using I AM for the desires. If revenue 'x' is one of your top three desires, your sentence should read, "I AM generating a revenue of 'x' in my business."
3. Catch yourself when your self-talk or conversation is not aligned with the above.

STEP 2: The Science of Repetition

Recently, I received a video message on 'WhatsApp University' about a miracle oil that could revive hair growth even in the baldest. It sounded exciting but did not linger long enough to acquire sufficient mind-space due to the incessant flow of such messages and receded into the background.

A day later, I received that message again. And again. This barrage continued for a week unabated. By now, I had watched the first minute of that video three times and the next minute twice. By day seven, I fell prey to watching the entire video length and spending time reflecting on it.

The brain is a helpful being. When any specific information byte is bombarded upon it multiple times, the neurons work to give that byte a sense of importance. It then starts making its way to the subconscious and, with persistence, is transformed into a belief.

Recall the famous old saying. "*A lie told a hundred times becomes the truth.*"

The next time your goals take the shape of significant employee numbers or multiple offices in varied geo-locations or generating enormous user traction, to bring them to fruition a pivotal lever would be that of **REPETITION.**

Repetition, then, is the *second most effective step* in penetrating the subconscious.

When a message goes through familiar paths and circuits rather than unknown territories, the brain creates patterns of recognition. And the brain loves patterns. These patterns enhance the release of a combination of dopamine and oxytocin (*The Art of Impossible* by Steven Kotler), the pleasure and love hormones, which sets off a chain reaction to cement the message that, over time, translates to steadfast beliefs.

STEP 3: Augment Repetition With This Special Cloak

Repetition per se may encounter blockages often. This is due to one crucial piece of the puzzle that has not been fit right— the dimension of **feeling.** *Nothing can ever transpire in our lives devoid of feeling.*

*"Only when you feel it will you see it." **Repetition** must be now adorned with the cloak of 'feeling'.*

Imagine an mp3 player in a loop with the phrase 'I earn a million dollars per year'. It will result in nothing. In that exact manner, any repetition of a desire will yield no result sans feeling.

Only if you incorporate the *feeling* of how it would affect your pulse, your heartbeat and your emotion when you achieve that hundred-million-dollar revenue target (if that was your desired outcome) with every word of repetition, will the result manifest.

So, the next time you venture on the repetition drill, ensure you have woven in the correct accompanying feeling around the words expressing the desired outcome.

STEP 4: The Time of the Day and Night

The brain has multiple wave patterns—alpha, beta, theta, delta and many others. They all are categorised and referred to as cycles/sec or Hz.

These have a predominant role in our lives, both at the conscious and subconscious levels.

The delta wave ranges from 0.3 to 4 Hz, where our deepest, dreamless sleep happens. Theta waves move in the 4 to 8 Hz range when you are asleep but can also exist when you are in a contemplative or meditative mode.

The alpha waves, situated in the middle of the brain spectrum, vibrate at a frequency of 8 to 12 cycles/sec. They are active when you are just drifting off to sleep or just in the process of awakening from a deep and refreshed sleep and they bridge the conscious to the subconscious[6].

This alpha wave range is the *Golden Frequency Band. The place where what you utter is akin to a command to the subconscious to open its gates and let the words enter.*

What you feed in at this moment is what you will program for an entry into the subconscious and, thereby, the belief zone. The early morning hours as you begin to waft into wakefulness and at night when you are about to drift into that cosy and restful sleep – these are the *bridging zones*. They form a seamless conduit to make the transition from the conscious to the subconscious – the alpha zone – possible.

As I had mentioned earlier, what you tell yourself does not have to be right. Or true. The power with which the feeling-infused words are repeated is crucial. *When done in this sensitive time zone,* it has the sharpness of an arrow piercing the subconscious. Let us move forward to the final step on our journey to reprogram the subconscious.

STEP 5: Duration

An oft-asked question to all of the above is, "How long does one have to repeat to be successful?"

How long did it take for the fake WhatsApp message to feel real? Apart from *repetition* and *feeling*, another aspect that constantly comes to play is the duration of repetition. While this has a lot to do with the intensity of the emotion (in a few cases, the intensity is strong enough to bring the belief to the fore instantly), it usually follows a specific time — *twenty-one days.*

Why twenty-one?

Have you ever watched a hen hatch an egg? It waits on the eggs patiently, providing warmth for a continuous 21 days. With full faith. Knowing with certainty that the eggs do not have a timer

that goes off after 21 days. But it waits. Be it a hen in any village in India, the remotest part of East Africa or the suburbs of Chicago, it's the same. The egg will hatch in twenty-one days. That is the unique magnificence of this number. Twenty-one. Whatever you choose to bring to manifestation, you cannot go wrong if the dedication is mixed with the magical number *21* in terms of time.
The ideal duration to ensure the repeated phrase reaches and penetrates the subconscious inch by inch is twenty-one days.

These five mightily potent steps create a small aperture between the conscious and subconscious, transmuting ordinary thoughts into powerful beliefs, helping generate that all-important quality, ***courage***.
There are a select few who have this ingrained in their very being. Today's legends like Phil Knight, Ratan Tata, Elon Musk, Jeff Bezos or Mukesh Ambani, who vibrate at that higher frequency, have either learned these techniques through their experience or have it inbuilt in their thought mechanism and self-talk, which they use effectively to create a process as their organisational template. Just like the erstwhile founders of legendary companies such as Procter & Gamble, Colgate-Palmolive and Johnson & Johnson who have instilled this thinking in the ecosystem of their corporations.

In the book *Power of Now,* Eckhart Tolle emphasises another technique that could result in similar and long-lasting results. According to him, by neither guiding the mind to a positive outcome nor letting it succumb to a negative result but being in the 'present moment' completely, you can handle the situation even more authoritatively.

Courage through Present Moment Focus

As Eckhart says, when we are completely in the space of the *present moment*, we fill the mind with power without the distraction of fear. That is the recipe for summoning up the courage to act decisively, however difficult the circumstances.

The potion for this recipe is MEDITATION.

Meditation is not mumbo jumbo or a complex game like many incorrectly perceive. It is just a method to keep the mind constantly on the thought *you want* rather than the thought the *mind wants* to lead you to.

Meditation prevents you from taking a sabotage tour into the land of fear but to a place where it matters and uplifts you.

Engaging in deeds of significance despite challenging consequences inherently builds courage. And meditation helps you achieve this.

A simple meditation technique can be along the lines of focusing on the breath. Count your breath in cycles considering one incoming and the subsequent outgoing breath as one cycle. By the third cycle, you will find the mind has taken a holiday into multiple other aspects of life. Great! Recognise that. That is the beginning of success. This awareness cuts the chaff and brings you to the moment. Guide it back to counting the breaths. The mind might once again wander. Reinstate it once more on the breath count.

By now, you have already attained over fifty per cent proficiency in the game of mind control[7]. This mastery is the core to achieving that all-powerful potion—courage. The ability to act as per what is demanded in a situation in a laser-focussed manner due to the steadfast mind without falling prey to any other thought. That would then mark the beginning of creating your 'new reality'. A reality that is fused with enthusiasm, energy, drive and power to know that there is possibly nothing you cannot achieve.

Having been privy to this all-powerful secret, Jim Burke, committed to 'Our Credo', immersed in the ethos of Johnson & Johnson, *believed*. Phil Knight *believed* and incorporated it into the thinking structure of Nike. The belief that they had in them whatever it took to surmount every hurdle that threatened them, thus, becoming *unstoppable.*

Persist in this exercise and regimen. You will soon reach that level where you have complete mind control, which is not just a prerequisite but also the *foundation for the courage* to emerge from within you. To be a Jim Burke, who could draw upon his internal strength guided by J&J's Credo. Or the P&G founders Procter and Gamble or a Phil Knight or a Steve Jobs and a few others. The first operative word in all their actions to ensure the Right Leg was anchored firmly was *courage*. P&G has also been symbolically referred to as an abbreviation for *Persistence and Grit.*

The formula is simple. Reprogram the subconscious to create life-expanding beliefs. Perpetuating beliefs lead to faith. Faith leads to courage, the most important ingredient in the anchoring of the Right Leg, the mind.

This enables a culture where warriors are constantly created in your company.

> *"Nobody has achieved anything big in business or any walk of life without* ***courage****"- Mukesh Ambani*

MANTRA 14

YOU HOLD THE UNIVERSE INSIDE YOU

Access the Limitless Undiscovered Wealth Inside Your Brain

> *The world's most powerful and greatest, yet least harnessed, creation lies in the space between your ears.*

This MANTRA will forever change the way you view yourself.

Kankaria lakeside, Ahmedabad. 9 p.m. A quiet night with a night bird occasionally stirring the air. The waters in the lake were moving cautiously in their own attempt to let the silence prevail.

It had been a satisfying day. Having delivered an impactful lecture in one of the top management schools on the significance of leaving the Earth a better place than we arrived on and living beyond our time through a legacy, I was in a reflective mood.

That is when I heard distant, faint footsteps, slowly becoming louder. As I turned around, I was surprised to see a young girl from the institute, taking copious notes during my talk, approaching me, looking somewhat distraught.

With some trepidation, she said, "Excuse me, sir. Apologies for disturbing you so late, but there was one burning question during your talk left unanswered and I really could not stop myself from seeking an explanation."

A little surprised, I asked her what it was.

Her question was along the lines of the clarification others had sought earlier. These are individuals who display passion and desire to reach the stars but get pulled back due to a gnawing sense of self-doubt.

She went on, "I believe that the process you enumerated to achieve legendary status seems flawless and we must leave footprints on this Earth that makes our journey worthwhile. But what if we are not inherently capable of producing these results despite all this? What if I am just an ordinary person with DNA that responds only to the lower frequencies?

"What if I am pushing boulders beyond my strength, only to be disappointed at the end of the journey, having wasted a full life?"

This is what I told her.

"Sheena (name changed) not only are your doubts absolutely valid, but I also admire your courage and taking the time and effort to resolve this. This act in itself will go a long way in your journey to becoming a legend. Having said that, here is something that will allay all your fears. Each of us, yes, every one of us, has over a trillion neurons in our brains. Each neuron is connected to another through a connector. The number of connectors in our brains is one followed by an incredible number of zeros. Can you take a guess how many zeros that would be?" I asked her.

She, half in bewilderment, said, "No."

"The number of connectors in our brains is a staggering 1000 trillion"[1] I said. "Our repository of neurons equals the stars in the Milky Way"[2] I then explained that this is a number not easily comprehensible even to the greatest of scientists. "That is the astonishing currency we each possess as brain power. Blessed and showered upon us by the Universe to behold and manifest the extraordinary. To transcend every act done up to that moment and continue to unearth something revolutionary constantly." I continued, "Everyone is already a legend. It is up to us to remove the veil of ignorance and self-doubt to reveal that brilliance."

Sheena was mesmerised. Then, as she thanked me profusely and walked away into the night's darkness, I knew there would soon be a shine akin to the diamond in the sky. A new legend was taking shape.

If you are harbouring a doubt even remotely like Sheena, remember it is time to discard it forever after this mantra of realisation.

MANTRA 15

DO YOU MANIFEST WHAT YOU DREAM?

The 5-Step Never-Revealed Blueprint of Visualisation

> *When I saw my dream unfold in my mind's eye, the world opened its curtains to showcase it in reality.*

The year was 1992. Jim Carrey, the superstar of today, was a non-entity.

Yet he carried with him a cheque all the time. A cheque for $10 million in his name for acting services rendered. Interestingly, no one had given him that cheque. He had written it himself! He had dated it Thanksgiving Day three years into the future.

Just a few days before that momentous Thanksgiving Day, he received a cheque for ten million dollars from a producer for the movie '*Dumb & Dumber*'.

There was this voice echoing inside him constantly that beyond the ability, talent and hard work, there must be a compelling reason for a small handful to shine far beyond everyone else. And one day, he had his 'Aha! moment'. That is when he wrote that memorable cheque that took him into history books and immortality.
For those three years, Carrey kept the cheque in his wallet and it served to strengthen his belief in himself with each passing day.[1]

When, finally, it materialised, he gave the entire credit to the **power of VISUALISATION.**

This MANTRA, probably one of the most powerful in this book, is to show the pathway, invisible to the naked eye, that has the power to bring every dream into reality.

Jack Canfield, the famed co-author of the legendary book *Chicken Soup for the Soul,* talks about a time when all he could muster was an annual income of $8000 and was filled with the desire to change his earnings track to $100,000 per year.
To most, this would seem ludicrous. But not to Jack. He knew the *secret* to bring about this transformation. Using this secret, he would close his eyes and visualise having a hundred-thousand-dollar bill in his hand and enjoying the $100,000-a-year lifestyle. In less than six months, with no significant enhancement in his competence or other augmentations, he received $92,327 that year just before the exact date. A bit short of the $100,000 mark but several multiples ahead of the $8000 he was used to.

He then turned to his wife and announced, "If it works for a hundred thousand, there should be nothing that prevents it from manifesting a million." This revelation then marked the arrival of his first million-dollar cheque from his publisher for the all-time successful *Chicken Soup for the Soul.*[2] He now knew he had landed on the proverbial words of '*Open Sesame*' but this time to unlock the portal to access the subconscious.

The secret: VISUALISATION

'See It Happen to Make It Happen'

This is the coaching programme at Nike, where constant visualisation techniques are encouraged to generate the best in people.

Visualisation has direct connections with what is happening in our brains.

According to Dr Sheri Dewan, MD, a neurosurgeon, when one visualises, certain parts of the brain, such as the frontal lobe (responsible for learning, planning and executing) and the occipital lobe (that helps to see what you are thinking), start getting activated in enhancing the physical outcome.[3]

It's no wonder that Oprah Winfrey, who rose from the depths of poverty to become a media mogul and one of the wealthiest women in history and Will Smith, the famous Hollywood star, use this all the time to literally 'create' what they desire.[4]

Brian Scudamore, a top entrepreneur and CEO of O2E brands, has clearly honed this technique to perfection when he says that he touched the magical $100 million levels from a stagnant $1 million only after discovering this robust process of visualisation.[5]

What, then, is *visualisation*? If it is so powerfully magnetic, is there a precise and structured method to decode its secrets that each one of us can deploy?

Fortunately, the answer is in the affirmative.

While many sing its praises, there are only few avenues where a systematic neurological blueprint exists, using which visualisation becomes an effortless reality. Since the results from this exercise were highly enticing and the need of the hour, I synthesised a system applying the gems of wisdom and principles from the masters mentioned above. But this needed to be put through the wringer of time and consistency to ensure its unchallenged supremacy.

In the winter of 2010, I put this theory through a rigorous test. What used to be the practice of the spiritual grandmasters of all time was now being advocated with ease by Jim Carrey, Jack Canfield, Nike and a few others who had seen amazing results. It was time that I ascertained its credibility.

The home where I grew up was modest, where the car garage welcomed and housed a bicycle as its permanent guest. While contentment was never in question, the dream of having one of the world's best cars there haunted me. The Ferraris did not catch my fancy but the BMW 5 Series was high on my list of desires.

To add to the excitement and enhance the complexity of this exercise, I decided on a specific registration number that I wanted this car to arrive with.

I unlocked the process of these giants and went through the step-by-step visualisation with rigour.

I set the date as February 12, 2011. And the miracle happened!

Around this date, a gleaming, dark blue BMW520d rolled into my father's garage to take its pride of place. That marked the day to confirm not just the possibility of manifesting the seemingly impossible but also affirm the theory that there exists a process so profound and powerful that it can turn dust into gold. What then can be said of transforming ordinary mortals into legends! This process essentially is the missing piece in the puzzle millions try to solve when they wonder why their arduous work and intelligence have led them only so far while the race was won by the few who seemed to have mastered something else. That missing piece, in one word, is visualisation, which has a unique recipe to elevate someone to new levels they could not have conceived.

Unveiling the 5-Step Blueprint to Master the Art of Visualisation

After studying hundreds of geniuses who have not 'made it' by traditional success metrics and the few seemingly ordinary who seem to have the Midas touch, it was clear that the latter followed a uniquely simple yet powerful system. A five-part, fail-proof method that, when implemented, would create such alchemy that no goal would be spared without turning into reality.

From the stories of Jim Carrey and Jack Canfield or the Nike program, one does not get the precise description of the mind map they need to use. Therefore, some may come to harbour the thought that visualisation is just imagination.

When it does not produce the required results after the first couple of days, they not only stop pursuing it but also walk away with disillusionment and condemnation or make light of this supercharged activity.

Hence the first maxim:

Visualisation is not another form of 'imagination'.
Not comprehending this truth has been the reason for the greatest misunderstanding of what this power-packed visualisation tool is about.

What, therefore, is visualisation?
Visualisation is a systematic, flow-transference mechanism, almost a science, that which triggers specific components of the brain to work in unison and manifest your desire into reality.

Here is that *flow transference mechanism* spelt in the most intricate detail.

Step 1: Specificity of What You Desire
In the anxiety to achieve our heart's desire in the shortest period, we all fail to be specific. Often, we create statements such as, "I want to have a fancy car" or "I want to be successful in my business" or "I want to be in the best of health".
The common flaw in all this is the lack of specificity. While the subconscious is anxiously waiting to carry out your commands, a statement like 'fancy car' or 'success in business' does not convey what exactly is required. It is hazy and nebulous. Business success, for some, could mean a higher number of employees. For some, it could be profits. For some others, service. Hence

the subconscious, in its state of confusion, chooses to remain silent.

So, the first cardinal principle in the land of visualisation is **specificity.** Suppose you strongly entertain the desire to possess a fancy car.

It is not enough to say you desire a fancy car. It is not even sufficient to mention that you aspire for a BMW. Nor is it enough to even say it is a 5-series BMW. It must be scripted with as much detail as possible when you are in awe of something you long for so strongly in the deepest corridors of your heart. It should be along the lines of owning a *5-series, dark blue BMW convertible*. That's being far more specific in detail. Then the subconscious has a definite order.

It is almost like ordering on Amazon. When you need to get those long-desired shoes for yourself, you do not type *shoes* in the search bar. Instead, you would specify the type of shoes, running or formal, colour, size and price range and then press the 'buy' button. The first step of visualisation is *precisely* that. Be exceptionally specific in every detail regarding the desire you would like to manifest.

Only then does the subconscious have a definite order to comply and deliver. And it will.

Step 2: Specify Your Desire in the *Present Tense*

This step is the most defining differentiator.

How often have you not expressed your desires worded in the future tense? Catch yourself when you say, "How I wish I had a company with twenty thousand employees!" or "I *will* achieve a growth of 50 per cent in revenue" or "I *will* create a business worth $2 billion" and so on. The critical distinguishing element is that the above desires are cloaked in the garment of tomorrow and *in the land of the subconscious, there is no tomorrow. There is only NOW.*

This knowledge is vital.

Because in the home ground of the mysterious, every act is played out in *this moment.* Not in some faraway time.

Hence your desire should be written in these golden words:

"I ***own*** a 5 series, dark blue BMW", "I ***run*** a company with twenty thousand employees" or "I ***have*** a garment business that generates a revenue of $2 billion."

The statement or command *must be set in the present.* That is when the churning of the subconscious begins to translate desires into physical reality. When written in the present tense, you ensure the words you utter are filled with the ammunition to reach the core of the subconscious. This is a secret unknown to millions that only a knowledgeable few harness.

A few more examples of scripting your desire in the present tense could be:

"I **am** the CEO of a company that employs 100,000 people."

Or

"I **earn** $1 million a year."

Or

"I **own** the most beautiful house in Bangalore."

The list is endless as to what desires propel whom. But the commonality is the way it is employed in words. *In the present tense.*

This method of structuring in the present tense is because the subconscious does not see the difference between 'what really is' and what you are '*feeding* it as is'. It may express an occasional sense of surprise when your income is hovering at $10,000 per year and you feed it with the words of your earning $1 million a year, but that's where *repetition* comes into play. Repetition enhances credibility with every occurrence. The subconscious operates only in the present and has no relevance to the future. Hence, it brings the necessary wirings and conduits in the brain to convert your affirmation into reality. Much like the computer with significant bytes of stored data, the subconscious, too, has unimaginable access to trillions of past data. Thus, it can work towards changing the present and not the future. Consequently, when you script the future as the present, the neurons in your brain align to open the doors of the subconscious, bringing the future into the present and thus making it come true.

Step 3: Fix the Exact Delivery Date of Your Desire

Let us revert to Amazon and the shoes that you wanted. You would be most upset if there were no delivery date mentioned for your order.

Similarly, in visualisation, to penetrate the subconscious and get it working, you need to provide it with an exact date. If your visualisation is "I own a BMW sometime in the future", then that 'sometime' will always remain in the future, never to unfold.

So, the third principle in visualisation mastery is:

Specify an exact date.

The key is to combine this date with a present tense feeling (Step 2). This can happen when you not only specify the date but feel that the date is **today**. This means if the date chosen is a future one of 21 September 2024, visualisation needs to be done with the **feeling** that today, *the date of visualisation, is 21 September 2024. Though the actual date of arrival is in the future.*

In words such as: "I generate an income of Rs. 100 crores by *17 August 2024.*" *With the feeling that the date of visualisation is 17 August 2024.* Irrespective of the date you are visualising on.

Or

"I have an employee strength of two thousand people by *15 September 2025.*" *Feeling the date is 15 September 2025, whenever you visualise.*

Or

"A VC (specifying which VC would add even greater impetus) has invested $10 million in my venture on *25 October 2025.*" *Ensuring you feel the date is 25 October 2025 all the times you visualise.*

That is a specific order to the online master of the Universe, your subconscious. And then the subconscious responds, "Your wish is my command."

Do This ACTION Exercise Now!

Write down your exact desire in detail with the precise delivery date and script the entire statement in the present tense.

Read it. Feel it. Now!

THE MOST CRUCIAL Step 4: Involve *Every Single Sense*

This step unravels the distinct difference between imagination and visualisation.

In the former, we create an image of the desire we want to materialise in the mind's eye. Which is great. But that forms only one piece of the jigsaw, though a crucial one.

What is as vital as blood and flesh that sustain life is to:

Involve and *engage every single one of our five senses.*

For example, let us now delve into the manifestation process of bringing to life your dream car along these lines.

Porsche 911. Is this your dream car? If not, substitute the model for your desired one and let us hit the road with this awe-inspiring step.

Close your eyes. See this beautiful creation in front of your eyes. The all-new Porsche 911. Its bright, dark, steel blue. Its hood somewhat raised. The wheels jutting out a little to grasp the occasional unexpected bend. The beautifully streamlined curve at the front. All these features merging into perfect oneness.

The car is a sight for the Gods to behold. Now you have engaged the *first and obvious sensory organ.*

Your eyes.

Stopping here would be akin to imagination. Your dream car will not manifest.

In your mind's eye, you now start walking towards the car as it occupies pride of place in your garage.

Remember you perform every act in the present.

Walking around the dream machine, you engage your second sensory organ. You glide your hand gently along the sides of

the car. The ice-cold metal makes your hair stand on end. You go a bit further and get a grip on the door's mighty handle. You adjust the side mirror and flick an imaginary speck off the windshield.
You have successfully engaged *your second sense.*
The sense of **touch.**

Now with one more admiring look at the length and breadth of this super vehicle, you pull the door handle and open it. As your eyes take in the impeccable cushioned white leather interiors, the **smell** of newness enters your nostrils and fills your breath with a sense of satisfaction. As you continue to take in its visual beauty, have your hands feel every inch of the car's grandeur and enjoy the new crisp smell. You have now engaged *the third sense* – **smell** – *even as you are revelling in the other two senses of touch and sight of the car.*

You now take your place in that most important position, the driver's seat and hold the steering wheel. As you conjure up all the driving possibilities of this new arrival, you slowly push the Start button. Then it happens. The engine turns on and that almost silent whirring is the most beautiful music you have heard recently. It's poetry in engineering.
Now you have engaged the *fourth sense*: **Hearing.**
All this while your eyes admire the plush interiors, your hand caresses the steering while taking in the new car's haunting fragrance.

As you continue to cherish all these, your eye falls on the dark chocolate bar your dealer has placed there to augur sweetness and pleasure in your life with this new arrival. You unwrap the chocolate and let it slide on to your tongue, feeling its silken sweetness. You have now engaged the *fifth and final sense*: **Taste.**

While not letting go of the beautiful vision around you, the purring engine accompanying it, you grip the steering with one hand and feel your back against the seat while the smell of new leather wafts its way through to you.

In effect, engaging all the senses *simultaneously.*

The above exercise, with a visceral connection touching every nerve centre in your mind and body, is the complete ritualisation of the all-powerful visualisation process, where *each one of the five senses is involved simultaneously.*

The Final Step 5: Feel the 'Gratitude'

This step has the effect of making the entire process up to now indestructible. And giving it a sense of permanence. Recall the grouting injected when the final layer of concrete is laid to hold the pieces together? This act of gratitude is the grouting of life. Your heart swells with joy when you bring the long-awaited dream to life. Now that heart should also overflow with thankfulness. It is now the time for **gratitude.** To thank the Universe for bringing all this together in a masterly symphony and producing that heavenly music. Of having your desire manifested. Thank the Eternal for delivering your desire and honouring its promise.

Feel that gratitude in every vein.

Once again, the *feeling* is the key.

Manifestation occurs only in the realm of 'feeling'. Without which it may just be a meaningless charade.

This five-step journey is the *elucidation of the unrevealed process of visualisation.* The *miracle voyage* that is sure to bring to the screen of your life every dream you intensely crave when you perform this ceremonial exercise. The reason it fails the ordinary is their ignorance of this detail or the inability to follow these rigours. When followed religiously, nothing can stop you in your quest for even the perceived impossible.

Do This ACTION Exercise Now!
Bring to life, using all five steps of the visualisation ritual, your innermost desire – to expand or create a redoubtable business, revive a stagnating or fraying relationship, enhance your health in an area that requires attention or bring forth a golden goose that will give you a constant supply of golden eggs in an avenue you most desire.

Thus concludes the miraculous blueprint of visualisation. An act, which when carefully and sincerely performed with the required degree of intensity for the specified duration, will never disappoint you.

When visualisation does not seem to work

It was a late Friday evening and I had promised myself I would be home early. But the clock, unaware of this commitment, went about at its own pace and was showing 8p.m. already. As I locked my office door, I saw a somewhat desolate Kiran (name changed) walking towards my office. Putting aside my urgency to go home, I asked him what the matter was.

He went through a barrage of reasons about how his visualisation technique was not working on revenue, the number of employees, a new office or the next sales order. Smiling, because I knew exactly what his folly would be, I asked him to detail his process.

He woes came in an outpour. He started narrating how he attempted to obtain a large contract from one of the Fortune 500 companies. He had closed his eyes and visualised the perfect product for the customer, making a powerful presentation on all its virtues, the R&D team incorporating the changes suggested by the customer to create an even better version and finally receiving the order.

I smiled again and asked him to pause, reflect and discern his error. Since he was unable to do so, which seemed glaringly obvious, I took the initiative to fill the gap.

I told him that his entire discourse revolved around the *process*. Only a tiny part was directed at the end to the contract's outcome.

Visualisation works one hundred per cent to the extent you engage and involve your five senses in what you ***desire****.*

In Kiran's case, he was spending over ninety per cent of that activity on the process, by which I mean product creation, R&D analysis and presentations. The *actualisation of the contract* accounted for only 10 per cent of his efforts. The Universe says, "Your wish is my command." So, the *process* in its entirety will materialise but not the outcome. Obvious! So, I asked him whether his process manifested in every detail. He jumped and said, "Yes, it did. Every element I had visualised in the process manifested itself. But the outcome did not."

I then explained that his visualisation of the *process* far outweighed that of the *outcome* and his result was in accordance with that. I then went on to present once again the clear distinctions in the detailed visualisation process described earlier.

Visualisation is about the outcome only, never about the process. The Universe takes care of the process. If you, like Kiran, were seeking to conclude a deal, you need to visualise only the outcome—of you receiving the contract document. Seeing it in your hands, with all the five senses engaged and feeling how you would *feel* if you were to receive the contract in reality. Remember, the subconscious does not differentiate between what you feed it and what is true. *What you provide the subconscious with is its reality.* But it must come with intense feeling. *Feeling* the joy of success. The ecstasy of having achieved something remarkable as if it has happened now! That is when dopamine, the feel-good chemical, will flow and *power and spur you* to achieve and manifest the subsequent desired outcome. And the Universe will conspire to bring together the people, situations and circumstances to make it happen.

If your dream is to possess that magnificent villa on the beachfront or an office in the most upmarket neighbourhood, ensure your visualisation doesn't go along the direction of only generating the required funds for the project. That is but one detail in the journey towards the final goal.

Racking your brains for debt or equity options, labouring through an EMI plan and visualising obtaining the funds and repaying them are only processes. Visualising these will manifest just that – the processes, not the outcome.

Visualisation is undeniably effective but works only where it is tuned in. Hence, the more you visualise any *process,* as in the above case funds for an office, the more that will manifest and not necessarily that dream home or the high street office.
Your visualisation antenna needs to be directed at the frequency at which *the outcome* operates.
I then proceeded to detail a visualisation exercise to Kiran with a specific example.

Suppose acquiring the most beautiful office on the high street is your desire.

The visualisation flow should follow this pattern.
"Today is the Inauguration Day of your new office on the penthouse floor in the most coveted avenue in your city. You have nurtured this insatiable dream of owning the most magnificent workspace in the sky. All your employees have gathered outside for the celebration with pride in their eyes. It is a bright, sunny morning, the sun's rays reflecting off the glass façade with signage that stands high above. The guest of honour arrives and the music begins.
"As the guests chant the congratulatory song, you and your dearest family members make your way to the centre and towards the red ribbon. As you cut it and confetti is thrown all over, you cannot but ***feel*** a profound sense of exhilaration.

You climb through each floor, taking in the grandeur, visit the offices of the CMO, CTO and CFO and walk towards the food court where the table is laid for the occasion. From the deck, as you look below, the deep blue waters of the swimming pool shimmer as you stand and admire the view. The beauty and the splendour of this momentous occasion grip you deep inside and you are overcome with gratitude for all that has been bestowed upon you."

You visualise all this *as if it is happening at this moment.*
With *all the five senses engaged.*

It is never the process, only the final outcome.
That is when visualisation manifests.
Kiran was astonished as he now visualised the glittering workplace I had mentally walked him through.
And here is the big breaking news! In less than twenty-four months, he was at my office again at a late hour, this time with a difference. He was beaming. He was holding a beautifully carved silver invite to his new tech-embellished office in the middle of the high street of Bangalore.
This time his visualisation of acquiring one of the top-end offices had become a reality.
(I did not mention that I too took part in an intense visualisation exercise for him!)

Do This ACTION Exercise Now!
Internalise these methods in detail and experiment with at least one visualisation process in the next thirty days, with all the five senses engaged, in the exact manner as specified.

MANTRA 16

THE LAST FRONTIER

The Extra Leap Beyond the Finish Line

> *When all is done, push a little longer. The embers will light up to reveal the fire that can brighten the whole universe.*

When all the diamonds are in place, they take on a superlative quality once they are strung on a thread. This act ensures the necklace can radiate a brilliance beyond that of the individual gems.

This MANTRA, then, is that thread. The one that binds all nuggets collected up to now while keeping the unique lustre of each intact. It is a culmination of the effort and determination to make all this flow in congruence towards the final symphony.

Focus beyond just the mundane: Your 'Sandcastle'

Robert was immersed in creating the marvel of a sandcastle on the seashore. A little later, when he lifted his head, he saw Adam, his friend, providing the final touches to another beautiful sandcastle a little further away.

All the enthusiasm and fervour Robert felt evaporated seeing Adam's creation. He instantly forgot all about his castle and started watching Adam, first with admiration and then with a sense of dejection that slowly turned into jealousy. His castle did not match up in beauty or size to that of Adam's.

Another hour went by. Robert's mother arrived to pick him up. In frustration, Robert, believing that his castle was inferior, kicked it down and left, head bowed in sadness while Adam continued to concentrate on his creation.

Reflect for a while on this incident. There was nothing wrong with Robert's castle. He was doing great. But suddenly, he let his focus get diverted to what someone else was doing. If only he had spent all the time he had squandered in envy on tending to his own castle, he would have walked out like a king, head held high, instead of drooping shoulders and listless gait.

There are times when hard work and effort may not yield the desired results, a moment when you may take your eyes off the ball, as they say. This gives rise to the view of finding the grass greener on the other side. Maybe a colleague, a distant rival or a competitor who suddenly appears to be on a faster path. That is when it is critical to keep your eyes on what you are doing more than what others may or may not be doing.

Hence it is good to remember that someone else's path has nothing to do with our journey.

> *Just because someone else is on the same road as us does not mean our destinations are the same. Do not race with them.*

Watch out for signs when you bring out the Robert in you. Resist the temptation to look elsewhere rather than provide the laser focus *your* project demands.

Pushing through the darkness

The scenic countryside of Erstfeld, Swiss Alps. The clock showed 1 p.m. as I wound my car through the bend and into the famous Gotthard tunnel, the longest in Switzerland. Driving there was an exhilarating experience. But only for the first few kilometres. Then something happened …

As I was driving in the darkest of Earth's submerged roadways I slowly started to freeze. It was a one-lane road in each direction, with heavy container truck traffic. Lights were hitting me in the face and suddenly, the 17-kilometre tunnel seemed like an unending hole of uncertainty. And the scary reality was that in this tunnel, there was no provision for any motorist to stop. Stopping would mean risking a collision or being hit by someone behind you.

There was no getting off the roller-coaster while it was on. I had to continue driving. Every kilometre suddenly seemed like an eternity and all the fun I had felt now turned into fear. I began to drip with sweat. I pushed through those nerve-racking minutes, which felt like hours and finally, when my car emerged from that famous tunnel, it seemed like I had been given a second chance at life.

We often may not have the choice to do what we want. But we are provided with another kind of choice. The option to build that internal power to manage whatever comes our way. Our focus then is not driven by fear (as to what might go wrong) but positive anticipation (as to what we might conquer).

If I had built that inner power earlier, my drive through that tunnel would have been one of ecstasy rather than trepidation. From that moment, my journey was one of consolidating that inner power and strength.

Everyday DO something that challenges you. Something that enhances your internal power, THE MIND. Create a 'today' that is better than your 'yesterday'.

The Transition from 'Great' to 'Legend'

Meet the most ardent cricket lover and ask him to recall at least four players with the maximum number of '99-run scores' in test matches. There is an extremely high chance he will fail in his attempt. Now ask them if they can recollect players who have scored centuries. The chances are nine out of ten that there would be a torrent of names in a moment.

Just one run crosses the threshold between obscurity and celebrity. One run is the difference between making one walk out in elation and achievement while another does so in despondency, frustration and despair. The irony is that it takes as much, if not more, mettle and numerous other qualities, at times, to reach ninety-nine runs in a test match as a hundred. It can be gruelling to spend hours gathering one run at a time to reach that magical figure beyond the nineties, but it pales in significance without that extra run that takes someone to a hundred.

Why all this attention and glorification for that one run?

The answer lies in the transition one must make from the land of the 'Greats' to the land of the 'Legends'.

Scoring that one magical run alters everything and you create history.

In life, we often confuse 'doing well' with accomplishing something that can be an exceptionally 'transformational' experience. In the former, there is a vacuum and a deep subconscious feeling that we are geared for more and possess a potential far beyond what we exhibit. However, either this piece misses our attention or we do not stop to question and redirect our efforts.

That is the story of the 'ninety-nine'; when we have reached a point where we may falsely believe we are at the zenith only to realise later that we concluded too early.

Why does this happen?

It has been found that the effort it takes to make that leap to a century sometimes equals the entire attempt to accumulate ninety-nine runs.

Let me clarify. The effort is not physical.

It is the effort of the 'Right Leg' that we have been discussing until now: *The effort of that phenomenal mind, the reason why the 'Right Leg' deserves such paramount importance.*

At the ninety-nine mark, the mind races. To some, the 'what ifs' of 'getting out' at that juncture invoke fear and thereby a higher chance of failure. To a few others, it is the glory of reaching that dream hundred which pumps the adrenalin and thereby creates a possible chance of spectacular success.

The true legends perform this task differently. They neither yield to the fear of failure nor the euphoria of success, as both are illusory and unreal. They fully recognise that the only reality is the ball of the moment, which deserves full attention.

These people have practised the art of not yielding to any thoughts leading to either emotion, fear or exhilaration. They have the clarity that either emotion has the potential to deprive one of the vital energies necessary to put in that conclusive and sometimes monumental, attempt to cross over.

So here is a crucial question.

How does one recognise one is at ninety-nine and not at a hundred?

Here is a quick check.

If you are in a state of mind, in any activity, where you feel you have accomplished that incredible feat and are on the threshold of a profound sense of achievement, that is when you must recognise you are only at ninety-nine and not at a hundred.

That is when your elevated journey begins. Yes, it's true. It would help, if you started now, to reboot both your mental and physical levels to a different high. In automobiles, a function called the turbo mode leverages the fuel injector to go notches above the ordinary, producing an entirely elevated set of results. What your business needs now is to go into turbo mode.

Pause. Look at the offerings, analyse the customer responses in minute detail, delve into the market statistics till every dot on the canvas is covered and reset new objectives based on the small space of opportunities this exercise will unveil. Then, jump-start your efforts and fire on all cylinders in every aspect like the product, people, technology, customer analytics, etc.

In the book *Good to Great*, Jim Collins classifies this as 'rinsing your cottage cheese.' It's a term for the discipline one should possess to squeeze every particle of what they have to bring out the last drop, leave no stone unturned.

Additionally, you need to further energise the Right Leg, the mind, through mindfulness and meditation to ensure this instrument is razor-sharp for the revised dynamics to unfold. This is how you get from 'Great' to 'Legend'.

This journey will feel like you are on the 1-to-99 road once again. But this time, it is to the land of the sublime, the land of the legends at which this book is aimed.

How does one know they have crossed the ninety-nine to the one-hundred zone?

This question is an oft-visited dilemma, but one that certainly has an answer when you seek it in earnest.

The earlier arena of ninety-nine would have been marked with a sense of achievement but lurking under the surface is a feeling of 'incompleteness,' an inexplicable semblance of a void. Contrarily, it is an exceptionally perceptible state of mind when you make it to the 'hundred' zone, one that reverberates with clarity.

It is a sentiment of undiluted joy and serene bliss where time seems to provide the perfect flow in a manner that tomorrow and yesterday have merged into that pristine present. A restfulness. A deep, inner satisfaction that there is nothing further to be achieved. That is the zone of legends. You know deep inside that you have 'arrived.' You do not require any external ratification.

Do This ACTION Exercise Now!

Stop and pause. Reflect on your present moment status. On your current business activity, your state of wealth. Maybe health. Or a relationship. In terms of your achievement, where do you stand? Are you at a 60 or an 80? Are you at a place where you feel an enhanced power to leap higher rising in your veins ?

Or do you feel you may be at a 99? What is your plan to reach that dizzy level of 100 and take your place among the legends?

Create a worksheet for all you need to do, as enunciated above, to stride to that coveted place.

> *Amidst the noise of the ordinary, even the whisper of a legend is heard.*

PART THREE

MANTRAS TO REMAIN AT THE TOP

CONGRATULATIONS!

If you have reached this far in this book, you now have the clear recipe to reach the top of The Golden Ladder.

Follow this meticulously and with patience. Nothing can stop you from achieving your goal of being a legend.

Create a manual of all that has been said in a structured, time-bound manner and implement it with dedication, determination and firm resolve.

Here is something you should *now* know!

> *"It is harder to stay on top than it is to make the climb. Continue to seek new goals."–Pat Summitt*

Yes. Remaining at the top requires an entirely new basket of *skills and proficiencies*. However, what distinguishes the legends is their ability, after reaching the top, to equip themselves with sound techniques that make them bounce back even if they slip so that they continue to *remain at the top.*

The following mantras will delve into that space and guide you to ***REMAIN at the top*** *once you reach there.*

MANTRA 17

IS THAT YOUR NECK ON THE BLOCK?

The Guillotine Test and More to Install You in the League of Global Icons

> *"What you do speaks so loudly I cannot hear what you are saying"-Ralph Waldo Emerson*

The MD of a courier services company, my client and I, were sipping our afternoon tea after what seemed like an unending, gruelling session on what it takes to bring out the best in leaders. Suddenly there was a commotion in the delivery section of the logistics department.

As we rushed there, we realised that a crucial parcel had been despatched to an incorrect address and the ire of the customer could be heard over the phone at a high decibel.

A blame game was being played out on the floor, with the team leader launching a spree of accusations against the person who was presumably at fault. We ensured that the first priority was to hasten the retrieval of the document and created a special service for its immediate delivery to the correct location. Meanwhile, I decided to try my *guillotine trick and requested the MD to convey it.*

The MD announced that as this was the third time this had happened, he would impose a penalty of Rs.1000 on the one who was the cause or Rs.500 on each team member. There was immediate and happy concurrence from the team leader, even though there were disconcerted looks on all the others' faces. At this juncture, I intervened and said, "As a second thought, let us begin with the team leader paying a penalty of Rs.1000." The team lead instantly started resisting. We then said we would revise the penalty to Rs.500. But his resistance persisted. The same person who was gleeful about his less fortunate teammates being punished was dismayed and agitated when the punitive measure was directed at him.

The MD was shocked at this behaviour. The team members' respect for their leader came down crashing.
This guillotine trick is a well-proven one to reveal the true leadership qualities of an individual. He who cannot feel any pain or empathy with the pain of his subordinates is the perfect example of someone who can never be counted on to shoulder responsibility and take ownership. It is a critical principle of leadership.

A true leader is willing to put his neck on the block for the sake of his team, making his way into their hearts and inspiring them so that they move mountains.

This MANTRA is that step to recognise 'leadership' and instil the needed qualities in your senior leadership team.

The deciding factor is one's ability and willingness to lead from the front, even in the most demanding situations.

Let us look at some of the top global leaders' distinctive qualities and how these can be integrated with your organisation and your leadership team to put your company on the map of greatness.

The organisation's first leader is you. Senior leaders who join your organisation will have to imbibe your values. The good news is that every single trait can be learnt. At any time. The following qualities stand out among the hundreds of top leaders I have been privileged to know, interact with and engage.

CURIOSITY: Every leader who has gone to an exceptional level is constantly curious. Curiosity connotes the thirst to know and learn and to become a better version of oneself. However, despite being curious, many may not make the necessary jump to greatness because of the intervening ego. True leaders hold their ego subservient to their hunger for knowledge.

SEEN EVERYWHERE: Be it the wedding of a distributor's son in a remote Andhra village, the birthday of a sales manager or the housewarming ceremony of a vendor in the interiors of the northeast during the rains, these leaders are there. Engaging with every stakeholder in their moments of joy and adding that oomph to the feel-good factor. While being there, they also ensure they understand their entire market and customer dynamics thus enriching their business.

APPROACHABLE: The few who remain immured in flamboyance, arrogance and other superficial attributes fall by the wayside in the journey towards greatness. The legendary leaders are always approachable. For everything. They take pains to ensure they do not come across as intimidating. Being accessible conveys openness that energises every employee and encourages them to be fearless and share all they want.

MAKE OTHERS FEEL FANTASTIC: You would notice many a leader surrounded by sycophants, revelling in their praise. True leaders do the exact opposite. They make the other person feel great about themselves. This approach breaks barriers and ensures the employees are constantly motivated to bring out their best.

DETAIL-ORIENTED: Every meeting they attend and every individual they meet is an occasion for them to be well-informed and abreast of the business at hand. This dedication not just helps them stay on top of things but also inspires the others to emulate them.

EMPATHY: This is the icing on the cake and one of the most important values I mentioned in the *mantra* on vision, mission and values. True leaders are deeply empathetic. They do not succumb to blaming and criticising when things do not fall in place. They focus on finding a solution in a calm and unruffled manner. Unlike the original team lead we spoke of, these leaders are 'on the ground' analysing every detail and furnishing all the support needed to arrive at a solution that will not just solve the current problem but also obviate any future ones.

Each one of these attributes can be cultivated. When you nurture these qualities focussing on the company's vision, you are silently creating iron-clad, strong leaders with the tenacity to go the extra mile while fully being empathetic to all others and their situations.

The organisations that endure are in a continuous quest to find and nourish such leaders.

Creating such a leadership template is a sure-fire method to become a recession- and adversity-proof organisation.

Do This ACTION Exercise Now!

Staying at the top begins with the right leaders in various verticals. Are your leaders able to pass the guillotine test? How effectively do they score on the other parameters? Compile this assessment for all the leaders on your team and set objectives based on where they should be.

Vet the leaders on these parameters and their ability to integrate themselves into your company's vision. You will find a remarkable synergy.

MANTRA 18

THE THREE MAGICAL WORDS

Service. Service. Service.

> *"No one cares how much you know till they know how much you care" –Theodore Roosevelt*

In the summer of 1995, I flew into Bangalore on a long flight from LA. I had no prior hotel reservation as it was a trip booked in a hurry. As the taxi wound through the streets, I chanced upon this glitzy tower that offered great deals as a hotel. I took a leap of faith and checked in. Room 1205.

As I walked into the room, I realised my shirt required ironing. Stepping out into the corridor and noticing a housekeeping lad, I requested his help. He pointed to a corner amidst the maze of rooms, where I could get it done with a portable iron. I hastened there, got my shirt ironed and left. But a slight sense of dissatisfaction lingered.

A few months later, I landed in Bangalore again. This time I checked into another well-known hotel where I had booked ahead.

As it was a Sunday and I did not have much to do, I opened the refrigerator to see what I could have. As I pulled out a can of orange juice, I felt it could do with some ice, which was missing from the minibar. When I spotted a member of Housekeeping, I requested a few chunks of ice. He accompanied me to the ice machine by the far side window and, after I added the ice, left. This episode was undoubtedly a better experience than the previous one in the earlier hotel.

In the winter of 2018, I had guests visiting Bangalore and I decided to host them at The Leela Palace Hotel. After the stay, Pradeep, a close friend, shared an incident with me.
One day, sensing a headache, he went out of the room to get a pill from the nearest pharmacy. In the hallway was this young employee who asked him if he needed anything. Pradeep asked him where the nearest chemist store was. After confirming it was an over-the-counter drug, the lad asked for the medicine's name and said to him, "Sir, you are a guest in our city. Kindly browse through these magazines while I get that medicine for you." Handing Pradeep the city's latest travelogue magazine and a fruit punch, he left, only to arrive soon with the required medicine.

This lad need not have done any of this. Like in the first hotel I described, he could have easily passed on the job to someone else and moved on. But he conducted himself entirely differently. He chose to paint the experience for the guest on a special canvas.

Acts such as this will ensure your company will remain at the top, like The Leela Palace and continue its stride. It generates what I call a *3x3x3 effect.*

If Pradeep were to pay even three times more tariff than the first hotel, he would still be willing. If he visited Bangalore on ten occasions over the next few years, his chances of choosing The Leela Palace would be three times more than any other hotel. He would certainly convey and share this experience with at least three more customers.

That translates into a potential of twenty-seven times (3x3x3) more significant revenue for the same service and product.

This customer empathy is the key to REMAINING AT THE TOP—the ability to go beyond the customers' needs and create delight while simultaneously providing empowerment to every employee and ensuring they deliver from the heart. Arising from a sense of ownership.

This MANTRA reveals the singular quality paramount to ***'Remaining at the top'*** *once you reach there.*

It is never about the heat outside, but the 'inside'.

Parts of the Northern hemisphere simmer like a cauldron during May and Dubai, despite being nicknamed 'the green desert', would still top the temperature chart. Forty-seven degrees C and rising.

The sales graph of the air-conditioner category usually followed a similar northward direction, but along with that came a baggage of woes.

On a hot Friday afternoon (a holiday in the Middle East those days), as I was settling down to take my afternoon nap, a frantic call from a local Arab national changed that. Not only had his air conditioner stopped working, his newly painted wall was now decorated with a design from the dripping water of the unit. The heat '*inside*' (mind) was several degrees higher than the outside.

This air conditioner was part of a new private label brand that I was heading and the measures I took at that moment would very well script its history. I was standing on the cusp of something new that would unfold.

Having the air conditioner removed from the customer's place within the next thirty minutes was elementary. A no-brainer. Which we did.

After that, I only have Peter Burwash (author of '*The Key to Great Leadership*' and Ron Kauffman, author of '*Up Your Service*') to thank.

Removing the air conditioner and reinstalling it post-repair, post-haste, was not why the customer had purchased the product in the first place. Often, companies misread this and feel that setting a defective product right and at top speed places them in the category of firms providing exemplary customer service. Completely incorrect! It was not supposed to go faulty in the first place. Period.

In this instance, the customer was facing the heat (both inside his head and outside), which he did not have to, only because he decided to buy the new private label brand.

So, the first action we took was something never practised, a rarity even today, in 2023. While we had the defective product removed, we went a step further. A small step but one that neutralises the heat of the moment. We instantly refitted his place temporarily with the best air conditioner in our stock so that he did not have to spend the next few days in agony and frustration till his unit returned.

Such an additional effort has yet another cascading effect. If this replacement had not been carried out, he would not just ruminate and create negativity for himself. He would also deride the brand in his head and be an extremely vocal devil's ambassador, conveying to a hundred others his plight. All a huge downward spiral for a new launch.

Through this one act, we reversed the entire narrative. While at peace with the heat, he would sing the brand's glory about how we had helped him. Remember, we did not help. It was his right to have a product in fully functional form when he paid for the unit. All we did was alter his thinking, aligning him towards the better side of us.

This approach makes a company ***remain at the top,*** *having reached there.*

For example, how many car owners or companies can claim their customer's faulty car is replaced temporarily with a new one till their vehicle is returned in case of a problem?

The story does not end there. To be that legend who continues to stay at the top, yet another piece needed to be fitted. We realised that and were ready.

When his old air conditioner was returned after the repair, I was struck by a great realisation. This entire exercise we had undertaken was for the customer, at best, to be back where he started. In the first place, a brand-new unit was not supposed to fail. By correcting the mistake, we had not performed a miracle. That was his consumer right. This lack of understanding is where most, if not all, companies stop and walk away feeling proud of what they have "accomplished." That is where they miss being on the train of legends.

If you have reached the top of the ladder and are now keen to REMAIN there without slipping, there is one more act to be completed.

That is *redress*. You need to ease the pain the customer has endured by choosing to buy the product.

Only a minuscule number of companies ponder over this issue and an even smaller fraction put that into action.

We needed to provide *visible and quantifiable value* that could mitigate the pain.

Recognising this, we embarked on a new initiative. Customarily, the warranty of any air conditioner lasts five years, but the product's usability stretches beyond ten. In the period succeeding the warranty, the customer incurs several expenses on service, which can be a financial challenge.

Recognising this difficulty we offered the customer an additional warranty of two years, totally free, which, while being a visible financial bonus, was not offered by any competitor. Thus giving him additional peace of mind. Along with that, a more profound and positively woven connection with the brand. The customer was truly delighted as this was a first for him. While this did not create a big dent in the company's pockets, it did forge a lifelong engagement with him. As I walked away from the customer's villa, I was filled with a sense of fulfilment. We did our bit to enhance the greenness of the Dubai desert that day.

Inside the Wheels of Hyundai

The winter of 2016 saw Hyundai launch a stunning new model that would soon take the market by storm. Eager to experience this latest entry, I went ahead and got myself one. As it arrived, its gleaming white contours shining, I was visibly excited. Unfortunately, within minutes the excitement gave way to disappointment as one of the front doors refused to close properly.

After much going back and forth, Hyundai did take the car back to set it right, while my mind was besieged by the discontent that I would receive a not so pristine product, one that had to be repaired even before it entered my home (like the air conditioner).

They certainly did not provide me with a replacement but what they did after they returned the car shipshape deserves reflection.

They realised they needed to lessen the misery I had felt in not having the brand-new product I deserved. They also recognised the importance of compensating me with a unique value for the agony of not having received what was promised, even though it was ultimately set right.

They organised a movie event where a few select customers like me were called to one of the top releases with free tickets and made to feel special at the theatre with designer seats and free eats, ensuring a unique and memorable movie experience.

A small price for Hyundai, but a game-changing event for the customer. It transformed the negativity associated with the brand into one of positive emotional appeal. An act which etches a lasting value for the brand and creates a sustainable and self-propelling audience.

Hyundai recognised this.

To set right a product, which was not supposed to fail in the first place, was starting from ground zero. You cement your place at the top of the ladder when you go the extra mile in discerning and assuaging the mental and physical pain the customer was forced to undergo.

This *customer obsession* is the daily bread of legends. It is no wonder that Hyundai is racing ahead in its journey toward being the top automobile brand in the country.

Do This ACTION Exercise Now!

Identify an area where you can go the whole nine yards detailed in this mantra and establish your dominance on service. It would be the icing on the cake if you are already facing a customer challenge and this process can be woven into it.

MANTRA 19

THE THREE SHIELDS OF PROTECTIVE ARMOUR

Traits to Bulletproof You to Become Invincible

"

It is not how high you rise, but how fast you bounce back when you fall that determines your true mettle.

This long-distance call would change history. While waiting an agonisingly long time to have someone provide the rare oxygen of credit for his company, the call he received was not the most desired. It was a call that shook Phil Knight completely. "This cannot be true," he told himself repeatedly. After having a long-standing contract with Tiger, a Japanese shoe brand, the fact that it could plot against him and pull the rug from under his feet was the last thing he expected. He reconfirmed the news he had heard on the phone just to be sure. But the man on the other side was clear. Yes, Tiger was looking for other distributors. Despite all he had done and achieved for them giving his blood and sweat![1]

To recall, in the post-war era between Japan and the USA, in the early Sixties, he had mustered enormous courage and made a tremendously difficult decision, much to the shock of everyone. To hop on to a flight to Japan, push for and obtain the distributorship of Tiger shoes, recognising all the perils accompanying that move. To embark on his long-cherished start-up journey. Over the following few years, he scaled the business close to an astonishing $1 million revenue, a truly remarkable achievement. All this was going to come to nought any moment. His whole venture. His big dream. All about to vaporise. And for no fault of his.

This moment of uncertainty, the realisation of the tenuous nature of his venture and dependence on an external factor, such as a brand owned by someone else over which he had little control paved the way for the long and difficult journey to establish a brand of his own. A brand that would defy all these vagaries and root itself in unshakeable soil. ***Nike.*** Stemming from the exceptional quality to rise from the ashes and leveraging a power that all possess but few call upon: **RESILIENCE.**

On that quiet day, History began a new page:
The resurgence of Phil Knight and the emergence of Nike.

This MANTRA embarks on the three most powerful Shields that you need to don to BE UNSTOPPABLE once you reach the top of the 'Golden Ladder'.

And the first of this is **RESILIENCE:**

The latent elasticity of our DNA that lies dormant but is waiting to be unleashed to catapult us to heights when we recognise its potency and awaken it from its slumber.
How does one harness this powerful quality?
Resilience can bury itself under lethargy or fear, mostly the latter. Only when these shackles are removed will it reveal its existence, let alone power.
Keeping aside lethargy for a moment, let us delve into fear. What is fear and why are so many powerless against this?

When your mind is focused on an imaginary future situation and generates a negative outcome (ironic, since the possibility of creating a positive result is equally open to you), *that is the definition of fear.*
The first step is to recognise this. That is the beginning of realisation.
With this foundation, you must *decide to re-create* a favourable option for that future event, which is a choice you can resort to rather than yield to the mind's harmful compulsion. Even if it sounds incredulous or difficult.

You step into the offices of a potential client, waiting for them to walk in for the tender's final discussion, which would be a significant breakthrough. In those moments of solitude, you have two options.
You could let your mind wander to the possibility of your price being too high or the client being inclined to favour someone else, which would ultimately mean your losing the contract.

Thereby making your entire effort worthless. A beautiful narrative to set your heart racing and fill you with 'fear.' An imaginary scenario. Created by the genius, **you!**

Alternatively, you could spend those moments letting your mind travel along the route of receiving the order, making you the largest supplier to the client and taking your company to new heights. With offices and employees worldwide singing the company's glory. This, too, is imaginary. Once again, painted by **you**. As you can see, both options are, at that moment, produced with equal effort from your side, irrespective of the probable outcome.

With one significant difference. The first option would make you diffident and nervous and potentially worsen the situation when the client arrives. The latter energises you to rise to greater heights and invokes the confidence and body language to inch closer to bagging the order.

The second route is one in which you decide to act in a direction despite your fear pulling at you. That will ignite the courage required and begin weaving RESILIENCE into your system.

To act in a manner that will consciously empower you despite fear attempting to bring you down. Thereby slowly helping you claw yourself out of the pit and reach heights few dare to dream.

Begin with small doses of this potion. In places of lesser consequence. With time, this will transform your brain and provide you with the right ingredients to accept increasingly difficult options and guide you toward a positive outcome, thereby making you ACT when fear could have held you back.

A semi-naked man was shaking and thrashing in his sleep, in an appalling environment at a remote and secret location in Germany.

As Viktor Frankl, the legend who defied all odds to emerge from the psychotic torture of the Nazis, reached out to wake this cell mate, he suddenly stopped. It occurred to him that however traumatic the nightmare the man was witnessing, it could not compare to the reality of where they were.

They were in Auschwitz, the concentration camp whose name was synonymous with all things horrific. In his book, *Man's Search For Meaning*[2] Frankl describes it as the place the worst sadists would find difficult to conceive of. It was not surprising, therefore, that even the darkest dream his colleague was experiencing would be heaven compared to the waking truth.

What made Frankl emerge from this harrowing place, where his sanity and existence were under threat every minute and become one of the world's top psychiatrists, psychologists and counsellors? Overcoming the incoherence of the insanity that prevailed around him.

He accords this personal resurrection to his recognition of *a meaning,* ***a deep sense of purpose to life,*** which he suddenly discovered.

That was to walk out from that hell hole, reveal the cruelty he witnessed to the world and undertake everything in his control to help people break the shackles of physical and mental pain.

One of his greatest quotes came from this: *"No one can steal my dignity unless I let him do so."*

One of the challenging moments you may encounter when things are going swimmingly is *when an unexpected storm hits and rocks the ship, threatening its very existence.* This danger could be in the form of the recent pandemic, Covid, that tossed not just businesses but the very fabric of humanity out of gear into the seas of chaos or a totally unexpected situation that comes out of the blue to challenge every premise you had set.

But the ones who remain at the top, contrasting with people who buckle under duress, have trained for this remarkable quality, *resilience.* These are the few who have ridden the waves of torment through decades but still hung on to the surfboard of the number one position.

*And **RESILIENCE** is that quality which forms the **first 'Shield of Protection'.***

Today's 'Apple of everyone's eye' in business had its founder, Steve Jobs, ousted in the first few years of its life despite the company's remarkable initial success. It was a company founded during the PC (Personal Computer) revolution, but Jobs suddenly had no place. In a boardroom battle between Jobs and the CEO he had hired, he suddenly found himself pushed to the corner and had to leave.[3]

But as the company faltered after his departure and bled in leadership, vision and money, it was forced to get Jobs back, although through NeXT, another startup that Jobs founded.

In those eight to ten years after his ouster from the company, Jobs did not go into hiding or fall victim to depression. On the contrary, he was constantly engaged in how he could create the next revolution. He was obsessed with that possibility and achieved it.

When he re-entered, he created history, gave the world the vision of the iMac, iPod and the revolutionary iPhone and transformed the industry in a manner that no one could even conceive of. Thus, Apple stands victorious today as the role model of retrieving life from the jaws of death. This ensured that he lived far beyond his physical presence on this planet. Today he is respected as one of the greatest creative geniuses who has combined that prowess of 'staying power' with business acumen. Although his time on Earth was short, he etched onto this world yet another **powerful lesson** to REMAIN AT THE TOP of the Golden Ladder. A lesson of **RESILIENCE.**

The extraordinary ability to persist in your dream regardless of all the hurricanes that lash and threaten to drown you.

Did you know that Netflix, the streaming service that captivates and keeps us stuck to our couches, come what may, was once a DVD mail-order service?

In a defining moment, as early as 2007, Netflix embarked upon the experiment of segregating DVD and 'video streaming'. But unfortunately, the DVD sales took a downward trend even as the streaming service began sluggishly. And by 2008, the overall DVD market fell by 26 per cent. The company, however, felt deep down that it was on the right path and continued with indefatigable persistence. And come 2011, when they segregated the DVD sales under the brand, Qwikster, close to 1 million subscribers left and Netflix was staring at a complete debacle[4]. But with more failure came even more persistence. It recognised its flaw of not speaking to the customer before taking a monumental action such as this and reversed its decision to arrest the downfall. (Lesson *from Mantra* 9). And finally, in 2013, its first original show, *House of Cards*, broke all viewership records and, in 2015, launched it into the upper echelons of media companies and the rest, as they say, is history.

This attitude is the power to persist. Constantly pushing ahead even if the results may not be to your liking, with the belief that there are astounding prospects in the future and the vital ingredient for that: **RESILIENCE.**

As we speak, Netflix, whose share price tumbled 75 per cent by May 2022 as content costs skyrocketed, has resurrected itself through this very quality of *resilience*, to RISE by over 100 percent in the last 10 months. Though it still has a way to go to regain its highs of November 2021, this attitude to defy all odds is amply evident in all its actions.

This critical element of RESILIENCE ensures you remain at the top of the 'Golden Ladder' even as it threatens to slip or your feet are unsteady. The uncanny ability to stick to your vision and believe in the ability that fired the idea in the first place while simultaneously ***finding meaning in your current state.***

Lockdown 2020. The world had shut all doors.

The streets, once a packed jungle of humans, were transformed into urban deserts. The world became a no-man's land.

Kabeer, the founder of Dunzo, talks quite nostalgically in his blog[5] about the five elements that transformed the company. Among them my favourite is about the time a Dunzo delivery boy was stunned as he walked out of an apartment block to see many residents applauding his courage and saluting him from their balconies after he handed over a critical product to a resident during Covid's peaking numbers. In an instant the boy was transformed from an ordinary delivery agent to a power-packed *warrior.*

The second instance relates to a time when there was a data breach in the company and what followed was a story unto itself for after-dinner conversations. The customer was livid. This data breach meant a colossal financial outlay and an immeasurable loss of face and credibility for Dunzo. This outcome was not something that the corporate client was prepared for and an event that could very well script its obituary since such classified customer data was of immeasurable value. One that could have irreversible consequences.

That is when Dunzo realised the true ***emotional business*** *it was in.* At that moment, it was convinced it was not in the functional business of transporting a parcel from one place to another. But in the hallowed and sanctified business of a different kind. *That* *of honouring the* ***TRUST*** *of their customers. (Essence of Mantra 4). Trust could take decades to earn but could be destroyed in a moment.*

That changed how Dunzo viewed everything. It could not afford to misplace or lose articles of the customers who placed their full trust in them.

The first act Dunzo did was to 'accept' the situation. Not defend it.

It went about setting the situation right when it realised that it only takes a heartbeat to lose a lifetime's gain (in Kabeer's words). So, it went through harrowing times to unearth every fault systematically, put its house in order and bring the *emotional quotient* of the business back on track—the quotient of TRUST.

This recognition called for a different kind of action since not upholding the customers' trust could mean a lifetime of irreparable damage for those customers and in turn for Dunzo. Hence as it got onto the first act of ACCEPTANCE, it set about re-establishing that crucial emotion of *trust,* which was its true business. That which defined it. This acknowledgement solidified its relationships and business far stronger.

In all these examples, one factor stands apart clearly. The true giants and legends who are ensconced on top of that Golden Ladder recognise the criticality of this essential element, one that separates them from the ordinary. Especially when circumstances are extremely unfavourable. When the world seems to be closing in on them. That is **RESILIENCE.** The innate capacity to push through every barrier when everything around them seems to be falling apart.

"Without resilience, there's not much you can achieve as a founder," Kabeer Biswas, Dunzo.

A day of thunder and lightning....

Early one eventful day in the early Seventies, there was a palpable eagerness in everyone at home. The results of my IIT entrance exam were to be announced that day. I was already a gold medallist in school and I only had to decide which IIT I would attend. As these discussions filled the room, the paper boy threw the day's newspaper, the breakfast of many, into the house.

I rushed to the verandah and picked it up to look for my results. "Is it in the top hundred?" I could hear my mother asking from behind. My dad would rather wait than predict.

As I started scrolling, my eyes could not find my name in the first hundred. That was not such an issue. But I did not find it in the first two hundred. Nor in the next five hundred. And not in the complete list of sixteen hundred successful candidates.

My first thought was that I might have missed seeing my name in the list as I started to scroll down again. Once again, no name. There must be some mistake. I looked at the heading to ensure this was the correct data I was looking at. Nothing wrong there. It then started to hit. "Could it be possible that I did not make it? Nah, how can that be?" I went through the grind of checking again.

The name was not there. It was evident. I had not made it. There was deep silence all around. A cloud of gloom seemed to descend.

I went inside, resigning myself to a future of enrolling in a school that would not hold my fancy.

I could hear my parents saying from afar, "It is okay, you can try next year."

"No way am I going to attempt this again!" This was the thought ringing through my head. Over the next few weeks, the irony slowly permeated through me. Here I was, a gold medallist from school, but seemingly giving up at the first sign of what seemed like a failure. But my father's persistence over the next two long months finally convinced me to sit the exams again. Of course, the gods were favourable this time as that same daily paper heralded the news of my success a year later.

Your entrepreneurial journey and the voyage of life itself will not be devoid of surprises. Or shocks! Some outcomes, which you may even have taken for granted, do not materialise and shake you to the core. This can throw you off balance, put you in a state of semi-withdrawal and make you question the very basis of the entire project.

That is when your awareness of a few critical factors will help you keep sailing and weather the storm.

As I mentioned earlier, the most powerful of all those factors is highlighted in Viktor Frankl's '*Man's Search For Meaning*' to anchor you in times of turmoil. The ability to '*search for the true meaning*' is the driving force for all you are and all you want to do. *Why do you really want to do what you want to do?*

This obviously is a challenging task, but nonetheless hugely important.

How does one search for meaning when everything seems to fall apart?

It comes from the lighthouse of your core values, which you defined and cemented in the second mantra in this book. *The reason the mantra of vision, mission and values is so critical.* These are the life-saving masks you can reach out to and draw new breath from.

You can revisit the values that define you and energise your current course or even alter it, if required, to align it with your values.

Like Jim Burke said after the Tylenol fiasco. Once he laid eyes on the values stated in 'Our Credo', his decision was easy and he could sell his action plan to everyone who mattered.[6]

The Covid pandemic brought to the fore the true difference that resilience made. Many businesses fell apart during that time, but a few resilient ones kept going, a few at an even more rapid pace.

In a time marked by chaos and depression, who could have imagined Mukesh Ambani would double his stock value by partnering with another overseas company in a completely new arena of retail even as oil revenues kept slipping?

Through this alliance, the man, not surprisingly, noted for his consistent and relentless pursuit in this direction of 'purpose' demonstrated what he stood for in a clear and visible manner.

What he exhibited during the telecom days of placing his faith in an entirely new and uncharted territory of LTE (Long Term Evolution, also known as 4G) was remarkable. Embracing the technology with a conviction that only a chosen few seem to exhibit, transformed the business into an industry unto himself in a surprisingly brief period with Jio.

Ambani derived this power from the purpose he sought for himself. Of not just making a small difference but revolutionising and transforming the world into a noticeably better place. That powered the unshakeable foundation of **resilience.**

These are the lessons in history that will seize the imagination of tomorrow's minds.

My friend Kunal Mehta (name changed) ran an excellent travel and hospitality company in Mysore for many years.

Come Covid and everything changed. Instantly. His business came to a staggering halt. All that he had built over decades seemed to vaporise overnight. That is when we spoke and he reflected on his core values. And *the 'search for his true meaning'*. That transformed his thinking. *His sense of 'meaning' came from the deepest desire to serve and see people happy.* One of the avenues was hospitality. But that was just one manifestation of his values. There could be others.

That is when he hit upon a new avatar for his business, where he converted his small office space into a fruit and vegetable shop and decided to use his network to leverage and benefit everyone. When the most basic human needs hung in the balance, he came up with a simple app where people would place their orders the night before and ensure they received them the next morning in all the areas that he could physically cover.

Remember, the ego has no place where values dominate.

This venture has evolved into such a success in the last eighteen months that he now runs a fully automated model wherein a large section of the population's multiple daily needs are met seamlessly and harmoniously.

"Seeing them (his customers) smile with a sense of calm and security about not having to worry about their daily needs is a reward I could not have asked for more," he says.

This is **RESILIENCE.**

To persist in your efforts despite calamities, however tricky, knowing you are moving in the direction of your true purpose and values.

The *next 'Shield of Protection'* is a time-honoured one that has transformed humans into giants but continues to elude many, especially after reaching the top.

The power of a 'Mentor cum Coach': *The second 'Shield of Protection'*

In August 2021, twenty-three-year-old Neeraj Chopra rewrote history. When he released that mighty javelin into the arena, which touched the ground at 87.58 m, the record books ushered in a new champion.

Uwe Hohn, credited with reshaping this genius, was his first coach and a driving force for Chopra winning the gold medal in the Commonwealth and Asian Games.[7] Uwe is the only person in the history of this championship to have crossed the 100-meter mark, a feat that remains unparalleled. The domain expert recognised something which no one had. He discerned that while Neeraj was excellent, he needed a different training to move to a higher echelon. It was a specific method of holding and releasing that mighty piece of metal while simultaneously reinforcing Neeraj's belief that he could be better than any human on this planet. An outside-in and an inside-out correction. *The two legs of the Golden Ladder.*

Both were something only someone at a remove could perceive. Someone who is not just a domain expert (the Left Leg of the Golden Ladder) but also one who could power the incredible mind (the Right Leg of the Golden Ladder). Someone who could make you '*believe*'.

That **YOU CAN.**

The essential recipe for 'Rising up' the coveted Golden Ladder.

Neeraj's first throw of 87.03 m was a significant achievement in itself. But for him, it still spelt inadequacy. He was made for the legends. Thus, recognising he was still at a 'ninety-nine' (Mantra 16), he rewired himself and pulled in all the reserve strength to unleash his second throw. This delivery touched that magical number of 87.58 m to give India its first-ever Olympic gold medal in the *track and field* category in over a hundred years. While this did happen under the second coach Dr Klaus Bartonietz, who too recognised and inculcated certain timing techniques to achieve perfection, it underlines the importance of a mentor or a coach who catapulted Neeraj Chopra from a 'great' to a 'legend'. *A coach* who not just recognises your talent but also builds on your belief to transcend the ordinary and enter the world of legends.

Even in the victory of Saudi Arabia against Argentina in the 2022 World Cup, the coach's contribution was amply evident.

Often, companies which have achieved moderate success hypnotise themselves into thinking they know it all. While the gruelling climb and the less-trodden path that reveal the treasure at the top are unique, the ability to *remain at the top* having made this climb requires a special glue in the form of a mentor.

Many wonder what lessons someone could teach a champion like Virat Kohli or Cristiano Ronaldo. But that is the thought realm of the average. These heroes know it takes every ounce of expertise from each corner to access that lofty zone only a few manage to touch. This is beyond humility.

Elon Musk, the rare genius who happens to be the world's wealthiest, is also known to learn from mentors constantly.

By leveraging paths less travelled through the millennia, they ascertain their position to ***remain atop*** *the Golden Ladder*, learning from the experience and expertise of a mentor or coach.

A guide who can spot the pitfalls well in advance and steer you through roads of safety, roads sometimes never travelled or trodden by only a few.

As Steven Covey says in his book *The Seven Habits of Highly Effective People*, "Management is efficiency in climbing the ladder of success; leadership determines whether the ladder is leaning against the right wall." Words of pure wisdom.

That marks the role of a ***coach and a mentor*** who can extract/ evoke the leader in you by ensuring you place the ladder against the right wall.

Running the distance in any undertaking could well be done sans a coach or a mentor. But using one would, without doubt, make for that game-changing difference between a 'great achiever' and a 'legend'.

How does one choose a coach or a mentor?

Having established the criticality of a mentor moves us to the obvious next step—choosing a mentor/coach. In a society with scores of individuals reeling under the pressures of career, health and relationships, it is natural to see a mushrooming of coaches. Making the selection task even more complex. At least, so it seems.

What constitutes the acid test when hiring and engaging a coach?

Three factors go a long way in ensuring that the coach/mentor you take on has the innate capacity to transform you and help you reach levels you may not be aware of, to show you where your awareness of yourself falls short in making the most of the unlimited possibilities.

1. THE 'X' AND 'Y' FACTOR MIX

The starting point is the coach/mentor's background—the X factor. Their education, corporate record and achievements in the space of *your* enterprise, i.e., the *domain power*. There are a few who harbour the belief that it may not be necessary to be equipped with domain expertise, but I am in strong disagreement with that.

While that may be a possibility on the Y factor, which I will delve into soon, at the core, having domain strength invokes respect from the mentee, which is vital for success. Accepting advice with the firm belief that it will be transformational for them is a necessary requirement for any student to make their way to reach historic heights.

The 'Y' Factor, which commands far greater significance than the 'X' and the one we have dwelt upon as the key differentiator (The Right Leg) is the ability to manage the one mighty tool in our possession, the MIND.

The mentor/coach must be someone who has seen life's challenges and has bounced back. Someone who can teach you the skills to navigate away from a storm of, possibly, your colleague having been promoted over you, of losing most of your funds in a stock market crash or losing a long-term contract or even of the business itself faltering for reasons beyond your control. Someone who can instil in you the much-needed adrenaline, get your company to generate the required revenues and bring calm when faced with a temporary inability or even adversity. Someone who can help you *persist* in the face of multiple failures so you can rise to the top.

This mental tenacity is the vital Y Factor and you must ensure the coach has BOTH these skills.

2. SPECIFICITY OF DELIVERABLES

It is now your task to define your achievement objectives and the time horizon for the deliverables to come to fruition in the *most specific manner*. The clearer your understanding of the metrics and their effective communication with your coach, the greater will be their accomplishment.

It could be as simple as being able to whip up an effective board presentation in 30 days or learning the nuances of penetrating a new industry or innovative methods of acquiring new clients in the current market or any other that demands your requirement. From an entirely different perspective, the deliverables could well be the critical factors needed to '*manifest*' an 'x' amount of wealth in 'y' months.

Whatever they may be, explicitness in the roadmap is essential for you and the coach to distinctly chalk out a program, monitor progress and enhance faith in one another.

3. PRICE VS VALUE

Remember, it is your life! Recognise the VALUE you derive since this is the most important investment that you will make. To a considerable extent, this value would be contingent on Point 2, but you need to be open to the *clear distinction between price and value*. Seeing it merely as an *expense* could lead to a postponement or even negation of engaging a mentor/coach. The accurate method is to treat this activity as an *investment*. And indeed, as your most important one.

This clarity will ensure that you not only make the correct decision to engage a mentor or coach who is attuned to your deepest desires but that you also have complete control over the value you would derive.

What next is the Shield to further cement your stay on top of the Golden Ladder?

LIECHTENSTEIN. The world's smallest country. The time: 6 p.m. A cold February evening. Glancing through the wares in a street-side store, I suddenly heard whispers and people staring at me. As I looked back, confused, my eyes met a young couple who sought my attention as I was in their way. I shifted, was favoured with their smile and a thank you, but was puzzled as to why I seemed to be the subject of everyone's gaze. I asked the store owner what the commotion was. He casually mentioned that the couple who passed me were the Prince and Princess of Liechtenstein.

Wow! What an experience! What a lesson in humility! As they say, *lessons are everywhere if we are tuned in to be the pupil.*

HUMILITY is one of the most admirable virtues one can possess, which yields some of the greatest treasures in life. Liechtenstein is no doubt the world's smallest country. But I learnt my *life's greatest lesson* in those snow-capped hills between Austria and Switzerland. So far away but so near to the heart!

HUMILITY is one cutting-edge factor that the achievers of the material world, in their speed against the wind, completely miss.

This quality can help people take stock constantly and enable them to have their feet on the ground, an essential skill in managing multiple obligations. More so when situations are not how you would like them to be, even as you dream with your head in the clouds.

Feet on the ground. Head in the clouds.

A lesson for everyone.

Yet another ingredient, the **third *'Shield of Protection'***, in the recipe to remaining at the TOP after having reached there is the **humility** that lets you pause for a moment and value everyone's opinion while keeping your confidence high. Humility is not about bowing to someone needlessly but recognising that everyone out there could have something of value if only you listen. This realisation makes you wealthier in more ways than one.

Now the trillion-dollar dilemma

Are you the entrepreneur unable to decide between entering a products business with the challenges of manufacturing, distribution, collection and all the associated elements OR setting down the seemingly easy route of creating an app for a service that may or may not exist and thereby lead you towards a valuation that will put your name on the next list of unicorns? While an answer to this question may not reveal itself in the next few minutes, it would be appropriate for you to look inside. Figuring out what your innermost desire is would be a great start.

Why do you want to do what you want to do?

Are you focussing on the cause or the effect?

Is **money** the cause for you to pursue this venture or is it an effect and an outcome resulting from accomplishing your innermost desire?

Is **passion** the motivation or will it be the end result of what you deeply cherish?

The conflict arises when there is confusion in recognising whether what you want is the "cause" or the "effect". As an illustration, if money is the cause for diving into this, it would be a completely different narrative than indulging in something you are insanely passionate about, where money is just a by-product.

Thus, an answer, which need not be obvious, will reveal itself from the above, but whichever path you choose, it will not be devoid of thorns and tears.

No lands are won when the path to victory is expected to be strewn only with roses.

In recent times, many so-called successes have been in the service industry, primarily tech based. Most of them, if not all though, have yet to establish successful profitability-based longevity.

But the most significant actors on this stage are still the **revolutionary product companies:** Apple, Tesla, Nike, Colgate, Coke, Amul, Omega, Reliance, Unilever, J&J, P&G and many other such highly successful ventures.

Whatever direction you pursue, the service or the product route, every single mantra outlined here will stand the test of time and set you on the legendary path of that glorious dream you want to live.

Do This ACTION Exercise Now!

On a scale of 1 to 10, how do you rank on each of the 'Shields of Protection' described in this chapter? Set a plan for enhancing it and achieving close to 10 on each 'Shield'. Set a date. And visualise the outcome!

MANTRA 20

...BEFORE WE SAY GOODBYE FOR NOW!

Are You the Lucky One?

There is often this thought that one of the essential factors in life is how you happen to be at the *'right place at the right time'*. The toss of the coin.

In common parlance, what people call 'LUCK'. Many believe that luck is a decisive factor in success. Here's my take on that.

The MANTRA of all MANTRAS.

YES, luck does play a significant role. But not in isolation or on its own.

That is the key. It works scientifically, mimicking the formula of the immortal genius Pythagoras, who gave us the Pythagoras theorem.

"In a right-angled triangle, the square of the hypotenuse is equal to the sum of squares of the other two sides.".

THE PYTHAGORAS THEOREM

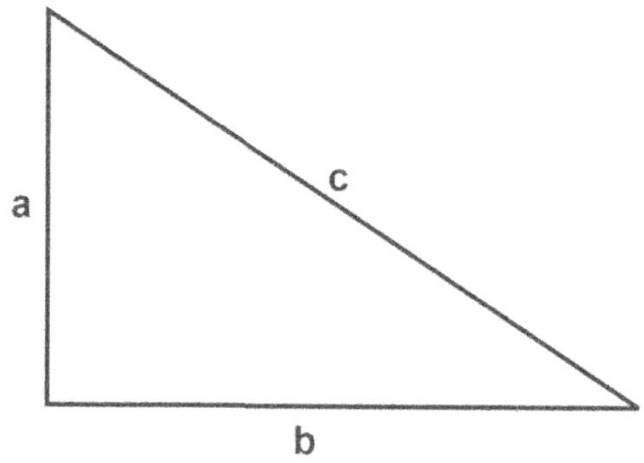

$$a^2 + b^2 = c^2$$

Here is the formula for incorporating luck into your unlimited business success.

Substitute 'a' for Left Leg, i.e., domain mastery and 'b' for Right Leg, i.e., mind power. The hypotenuse 'c' would then be LUCK.

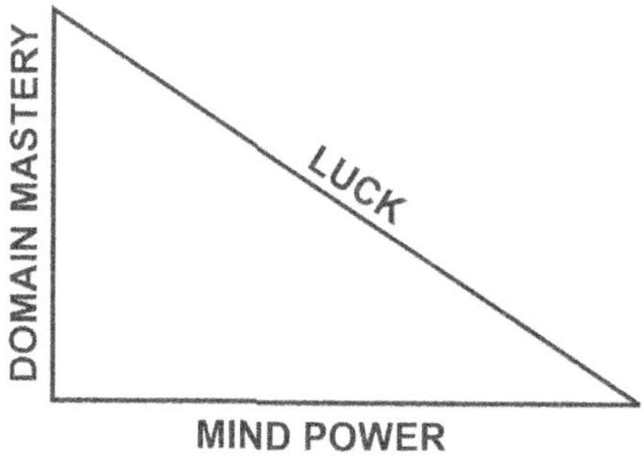

$$(\text{DOMAIN MASTERY})^2 + (\text{MIND POWER})^2 = (\text{LUCK})^2$$

$(\text{DOMAIN MASTERY})^2 + (\text{MIND POWER})^2 = (\text{LUCK})^2$

So, if you want Lady Luck to shine on you, ensure BOTH the legs of the Golden Ladder, in this case, in *equal quantities,* are anchored. This enables the Universe to bring the third factor of LUCK to shine in that proportionate manner. You will then have the complete triangle that brings all the aspects of your life together in perfect unison. To deliver the best you deserve.

So that you can FEEL IT and SHINE.

Here is wishing you all the luck in the world.

MANTRA 21

FINALLY, THE BEGINNING

Cement Yourself at the Top of 'The Golden Ladder'

"

If you keep doing the same thing, you will keep getting more of what you have already got.

I meet a large ensemble of enthusiasts on my various conference and workshop sojourns. Individuals who take on the occasional and sometimes regular 'motivational shot' to get that temporary high. And do nothing after that. Until the next workshop, followed by a whirlwind high again, only to be back to doing nothing rather than taking the wisdom forward.

Having touched the magical high of completing this book, which is a treatise to entering and staying in the zone of the impossible and the 'Land of the Legends', **the real journey begins now.**

The responsibility is now squarely on you. In your hands. Now, onto your feet! Move! Commit to following every step outlined in the book with a determination to be in the annals of the legends.

So, your voyage call has been announced. The mooring rope of your ship has been unfastened. You are about to sail. You are the captain.
All the controls are now entirely at your disposal. All it requires from you is to enable and use them.
Your destination is clear. There may be winds and storms along the way. But you are equipped with the necessary gear and gadgets.
Most importantly, you have also been put through a regimen for the rigorous mastery of the most potent instrument on the planet—*the mind*. You are also now privileged to have been provided with the instruction manual for it, to which the millions around you have not been fortunate to have access.
So, it is now time to **take on the world**.
And be the **ultimate master of your destiny**.
To leave a footprint on the planet that the world can forever see.
Be that incredible one whose shine matches that of a diamond in the sky!

This MANTRA is about the final call for you to step on the accelerator while simultaneously releasing the handbrake. The handbrake of lethargy. On to the highway of miracles.

The road to the extraordinary is no more shrouded in mystery. This book has unveiled all the secrets. No doubt, the path is not an easy one. But one thing is certain. It is not restricted to the land of the privileged few born with a golden spoon.

It may be worthwhile to highlight that this journey has been accomplished by many who were considered 'average' and some even thwarted by society but chose to 'RISE' to these levels because of their tenacity and by following the principles enunciated in this book meticulously.

They are the ones who dared.

They were not deterred by the immensity of the mountain that stood facing them but recognised that the journey begins with the first step and one step at a time.

It's not that they did not feel fear. But they chose to push through the fear, knowing that beyond fear lay the land of the fabled.

You can do it too!

Along the way, they also recognised the need for a path they could create for others to follow in their footsteps and reach where they did.

This they did, not by clearing the path of stones, but by putting together a dossier of the navigation methods to overcome every obstacle and hurdle.

You are holding that dossier in your hands.

If you harbour the desire to be legendary, nothing has ever been easier.

All it requires is for you to choose. To decide. And then use the template provided to master the voyage.

DON'T LET ANYTHING STOP YOU. From being the legend, you deserve to be.

TODAY is the day! NOW is the time!

Never again will you question why only some make it to the top and why you may not be one of those select few.

Your time has come. To show the world who you truly are.

RISE. TO BE UNSTOPPABLE. NOW!

A BIG THANK YOU!

REFERENCES

The Momentous Flight:

1. Dramatisation: Phil Knight. (2018) *Shoe Dog*. UK: Simon & Schuster.

Mantra 2: Far Away on the Distant Horizon

1. Johnson & Johnson corporate website: *https://www.jnj.com*
2. Nike Vision & Mission Statement 2022: *FourWeekMBA*
3. Apple's Vision Statement: *Business Strategy Hub*
4. Our Credo: Johnson & Johnson corporate website: *https://www.jnj.com*
5. Disney Vision Statement: *panmore.com*
6. Colgate Vision Statement: CEO Welcome Letter | *Colgate-Palmolive-https://www.colgatepalmolive.com*
7. P&G Vision Statement: *https://panmore.com*
8. Google Vision Statement: *https://comparably.com*
9. Tata Vision Statement: *Tatainternational.com*
10. Nike Mission Statement: *FourweekMBA.com*
11. Apple Mission Statement: *Apple Mission Statement, Vision, & Core Values: Business Strategy Hub*
12. Google Mission Statement: *about.google*
13. P&G Mission Statement: *panmore.com*
14. Tata Mission Statement: *Tatainternational.com*
15. Colgate-Palmolive Values: *Colgatepalmolive.com*
16. Google Values: *about.google*
17. Tata Values: *Tata International.com*
18. P&G Values: *https://in.pg.com*

19. Apple Values: *Business Strategy Hub*
20. Nike Values: *Business Strategy Hub*
21,22. Jack Welch. (2005) *Winning*. New York: Harper Collins

Mantra 4: What Business Are We Really In?

1. Brand Value, Coca-Cola: *Statista.com*
2. Feelings First: *Dr. Baba Shiv, Insights by Stanford Business 2020*
3. 'From Promotion to Emotion': *Connecting B2B Customers to Brands - Sam Nathan, Karl Schmidt October 2013*
4. The five most important emotions in B2B marketing today: *Jane Deehan*, August 17,2020 LinkedIn blog

Mantra 6: Your Baby's Umbilical Cord Tugs Here

1. RIES' Pieces of Slogan Savvy: *https://adage.com/article/al-ries/ries-pieces-slogan-savvy/127466*
2. McDonald's: *Repetitions in McDonald's Slogan Amar Fadilah1, Tatan Tawami2, ELTICS Journal Vol 5, No 2 Month 202*

Mantra 7: The New A.R.T. On the Canvas

1. Transference: *Brian Feldman's conceptual show, 'Dishwasher' - Orlando Weekly*

Mantra 9: Thinking at the EDGE of the Box

1. Dove, Real Beauty: *YouTube-Dove Real Beauty Sketches: You are more beautiful than 'You Think'.*
2. Febreze case study: *How 'Design Thinking' transformed 'Febreze' into a $1 Billion Brand, Shah Mohammed, June 8, 2017.*

3. IKEA Values statement: *"Why Do Company Culture and Company Values Matter?" | https://blog.trello.com*
4. Co-creation: *Researcher Aric Rindfleisch & Matt 'O' Hern. https://aspire.io/blog/what-is-co-creation*

Mantra 10: Money. Money. Money

1. Narayana Murthy: *Financial Express, June 4, 2022*

Mantra 11: The Golden Assets Club

1. Bruce H. Lipton: brucelipton.com *'What are the Volts of Electricity in Human Body?', Sep12,2022*
2. Steven Kotler. (2021) *The Art of Impossible.* New York: Harper Collins.
3. Spencer Silver & Art Fry: *Lemelson-MIT*
4. Steven Kotler. (2021) *The Art of Impossible*. New York: Harper Collins.

Mantra 12: Are You Hearing a No Whenever You Say YES?

1. Roger Fisher, William Ury, Bruce Patton. (2011) *Getting to Yes*. Boston: Houghton Mifflin.

Mantra 13: Inside the Vault of Riches

1. The Tylenol Killings: *Wikipedia. Judith Rehak, New York Times, March 2002*
2. The Courage to be Uncomfortable: *David Taylor, P&G, LinkedIn 2018*
3. Courage to say 'Yes': *Marc Pritchard, CMO, P&G, Cannes 2012*
4. 'Smile Above the Odds': *Colgate's campaign. Adage.com. April 2021*

5. Tesla Values*: Why do company culture and company values matter-https://blog.trello.com, May 2022*
6. Brainwaves: *https://nhahealth.com/brainwaves-the-language/#:~:text=The%20raw%20EEG%20has%20usually,)%20for%20%E2%80%9Cactive%E2%80%9D%20intelligence.*
7. Eckhart Tolle. (2005) *Power of Now.* Great Britain: Hodder & Stoughton.

Mantra 14: You Hold the Universe Inside You

1. Basic Neural Units of the Brain: *Cornell University, https://arxiv.org/abs/1906.01703*
2. Nature: How to Map the Brain: *https://www.nature.com/articles/d41586-019-02208-0*

Mantra 15: Do You Manifest What You Dream?

1. *Jim Carrey: $10Mn. Cheque, YouTube: https://www.youtube.com/watch?v=3s9AXLlKeW4*
2. Rhonda Byrne. (2006) *The Secret.* Oregon: TS Publications.
3. 'See It Happen to Make It Happen': *nike.com/stories/coaching*
4. Oprah Winfrey, Will Smith: *mindbodygreen.com. 2015*
5. Brian Scudamore: *inc.com-empact*

Mantra 19: The Three Shields of Protection

1. Dramatisation of *Shoe Dog*, Phil Knight. (2018) UK: Simon & Schuster
2. Viktor Frankl. (1984) *Man's Search for Meaning.* New York: Simon & Schuster.
3. Steve Jobs: *Wikipedia*

4. Netflix:
   i) *https://www.cnbc.com/2019/11/08/the-death-of-the-dvd-why-sales-dropped-more-than-86percent-in-13-years.html*
   ii) *https://www.inc.com/tech-blog/netflix-kills-qwikster-after-1-million-subscribers-leave.html*
5. Dunzo reflections: Kabeer, Founder. Blog
6. Wharton School of Publishing, *'Lasting Leadership -What you can learn from the top twenty-five business heads. Jim Burke: https://knowledge.wharton.upenn.edu/article/lasting-leadership-lessons-from-the-25-most-influential-business-people-of-our-times/*
7. Neeraj Chopra Coach: *Uwe Huhn influence on Neeraj Chopra, The Hindu, 7, August 2021*

Printed in Great Britain
by Amazon

41307201R00172